Ernst & Young's Financial Planning Essentials

Ernst & Young's Financial Planning Essentials

Robert J. Garner

Robert B. Coplan

Martin Nissenbaum

Barbara J. Raasch

Charles L. Ratner

John Wiley & Sons, Inc.

New York • Chichester • Weinheim • Brisbane • Singapore • Toronto

In the preparation of this book, every effort has been made to offer the most current, correct, and clearly expressed information possible. Nonetheless, inadvertent errors can occur, and tax rules and regulations often change.

Further, the information in the text is intended to afford general guidelines on matters of interest to everyone. The application and impact of tax laws and financial matters can vary widely, however, from case to case, based upon the specific or unique facts involved. Accordingly, the information in this book is not intended to serve as legal, accounting, or tax advice. Readers are encouraged to consult with professional advisors for advice concerning specific matters before making any decision, and the author and publishers disclaim any responsibility for positions taken by taxpayers in their individual cases or for any misunderstanding on the part of readers.

Tables of the following: Investment Mix—Expected Return, Standard Deviation; Low-Medium-High Risk on Asset Allocation for Young, Mid-Life Individuals, Preretired, and Retired Individuals; Historical Average Returns; Value of $1 Invested in Various Assets; and Comparing Two Portfolios that appear in Chapter 4 of this book are © *Stocks, Bonds, Bills, and Inflation*™, Ibbotson Associates. Chicago (annually updates work by Roger G. Ibbotson and Rex A. Sinquefield). Used with permission. All rights reserved.

The text is printed on acid-free paper.∞

This publication is designed to provide accurate and authoritative information in regard to the subject matter covered. It is sold with the understanding that the publisher is not engaged in rendering legal, accounting, or other professional services. If legal advice or other expert assistance is required, the services of a competent professional person should be sought.

ISBN 0-471-31644-X

Printed in the United States of America.

10 9 8 7 6 5 4 3 2 1

CONTENTS

INTRODUCTION

For most people financial planning is a challenge. Resources are limited and needs can seem endless. As with most challenges, achieving financial security is very much a matter of understanding concepts, organizing information, and developing a workable process. Rather than thinking about financial planning as a one-time activity, at Ernst & Young we think of financial planning as a series of steps that will help you reach the goals you set for yourself.

WHY DO FINANCIAL PLANNING?

While you can never predict how life's uncertainties will affect your financial well being, you can anticipate problems and take advantage of opportunities. You can save money and invest wisely. You can protect your family through estate planning and purchasing insurance. Financial planning can help you strengthen your control over the impact that life's "curve balls" can have on you and your family's finances.

Consider retirement planning. Like most people, you probably look forward to enjoying your retirement years. However, you may be unsure about how and when you'll accomplish this goal. How much money will you need each year? What happens if you outlive your resources? To what degree will Social Security supplement your own retirement savings? These are difficult questions. But careful financial planning can help you size up your individual situation, calculate what you need for retirement, analyze sources of income and means of investment, and design a plan to meet your short- and long-term goals.

Divorce is another example. No one would deny that it's an emotional event; however, it's also a financial event. Many people acknowledge the financial issues, but few see financial planning as part of their response to an impending divorce. Unfortunately, ignoring the situation can have far reaching, significant effects, while good financial planning can help secure the future.

In short, financial planning gives you options for dealing with the future. There are many ways to approach financial planning. Some people feel more comfortable receiving their information from books. Some like to use computer software programs. Others prefer watching financial planning videos, attending seminars, or seeking help from a personal financial planner. What matters most is that you take an active role in managing your finances.

OUR APPROACH

We've created *Ernst & Young's Financial Planning Essentials* to help you take charge of your finances. This book introduces the fundamentals of financial planning. It will help you set your goals, understand investment vehicles and concepts, develop and implement a strategy, and monitor your investments. Important tax issues are also addressed, along with such other traditional financial planning disciplines as investments, insurance, and estate planning. The overview that *Ernst & Young's Financial Planning Essentials* provides will give you the basic information you need to take action.

THE ERNST & YOUNG DIFFERENCE

Ernst & Young's long-standing expertise in the field of financial planning sets it apart from others in the field. For many decades, our specialists have counseled a wide range of clients—from individuals and couples, to small businesses, to employee groups of some of the major corporations in America—about retirement, investments, insurance, estate taxes, and all other financial planning disciplines. This book reflects our collective knowledge and experience.

RECENT ISSUES

The Taxpayer Relief Act of 1997 became law in August 1997. As part of this Act, changes were made in the tax law that influence not only how you file your taxes but also how you conduct financial planning throughout your life. Significant revisions were made to the laws governing paying for college, the tax impact of selling a home, and Individual Retirement Accounts (IRAs).

Incorporated into this text are explanations of these new provisions and what you need to know in order to make sound financial decisions. Among the highlights of the Act:

- Education IRAs
- Deductible IRAs
- Roth IRAs
- Long-term capital gains
- Treatment of home sales

The IRS Restructuring and Reform Act of 1998 modified many of the provisions of the Taxpayer Relief Act. Those modifications are also incorporated in the text.

REGAINING CONTROL, PROVIDING FOR THE FUTURE

Financial planning is, first and foremost, a way to build for a secure financial future and deal effectively with ongoing financial needs. It's not a cure-all. Rather, it's a disciplined way of achieving control and providing for yourself and your family in an organized manner.

Our hope is that *Ernst & Young's Financial Planning Essentials* will serve you well in meeting *all* your financial goals.

TAKING CHARGE OF
THE FINANCIAL PLANNING
PROCESS

If you're concerned with keeping control of your financial future, you have lots of company. Investments, inflation, taxes, and other money matters concern nearly everyone. Yet even if you recognize the importance of financial planning, you may have trouble taking action, sizing up your situation, and putting all the pieces of a plan together. You may find the planning process itself difficult. You may have trouble following the plan you've created. Or you may feel unsure even where to begin.

Ernst & Young's Financial Planning Essentials will help you take control of your finances, determine which financial goals best suit your purposes, and plan to meet those goals for your own well-being and your family's as well. If you're completely new to financial planning, we'll give you a method for getting started. If you have some ideas but no clear sense of how to coordinate them, we'll suggest ways to develop those ideas into a consistent, comprehensive financial plan. And even if you've already designed a plan, we'll explain how you can make it better.

First, however, you should take stock of your situation, determine your financial strengths and weaknesses, and start to decide what you want from financial planning. Chapter 1 is a starting point for everything else in this book—a sequence of steps for taking charge of the financial planning process.

These are the steps:

- *Step 1*: Determine where you are financially.
- *Step 2*: Set goals.
- *Step 3*: Develop a plan.
- *Step 4*: Keep simple records.
- *Step 5*: Make an informal budget.
- *Step 6*: Deal with shortfalls, credit, and debt.
- *Step 7*: Review your progress.

 # DETERMINE WHERE YOU ARE FINANCIALLY

Your current financial position is the starting point from which you should measure progress toward your financial goals. To understand your financial position, however, you need a practical means for taking stock of the situation. A standard device for this purpose is the *net worth worksheet*. This worksheet allows you to estimate your assets and liabilities as a first step to financial planning.

> **Net worth:** *what's left after you subtract your liabilities from your assets.*

Calculating Your Net Worth

Take a few moments to complete the net worth worksheet below. As you fill it in, make sure that you indicate your assets in terms of their current fair market value, not in terms of what you paid for them. For example, let's say that 5 years ago you bought some shares of stock for $1,000. That stock is now worth $2,000 (i.e., its current fair market value is $2,000). Put $2,000 rather than $1,000 on the worksheet. Similarly, you should assess the value of any real estate you own as accurately as possible. One way of doing so is to check with local real-tors for the recent sale prices of properties similar to yours.

One final consideration before you fill in the worksheet: This is *not* a financial "report card." There are no right or wrong answers. Don't be judgmental of yourself as you assess your situation. What you discover as you calculate your net worth may or

YOUR NET WORTH AS OF _____

ASSETS

Cash equivalents

Checking accounts	$_____
Savings accounts	_____
Money market accounts	_____
Money market fund accounts	_____
Certificates of deposit	_____
U.S. Treasury bills	_____
Cash value of life insurance	_____
Total	$_____

Investments

Stocks	_____
Bonds	_____
Mutual fund investments	_____
Partnership interests	_____
Other investments	_____
Total	$_____

Retirement funds

Pension (present lump-sum value)	_____
IRAs and Keogh accounts	_____
Employee savings plans (e.g., 401(k), SEP, ESOP)	_____
Total	$_____

Personal assets

Principal residence	$_____
Second residence	_____
Collectibles/art/ antiques	_____
Automobiles	_____
Home furnishings	_____
Furs and jewelry	_____
Other assets	_____
Total	$_____
Total assets	$_____

LIABILITIES

Charge account balances	_____
Personal loans	_____
Student loans	_____
Auto loans	_____
401(k) loans	_____
Investment loans (margin, real estate, etc.)	_____
Home mortgages	_____
Home equity loans	_____
Alimony	_____
Child support	_____
Life insurance policy loans	_____
Projected income tax liability	_____
Other liabilities	_____
Total liabilities	$(_____)
Net worth	$_____

may not please you; you may come away from the exercise either reassured about your financial situation or concerned about it. *But only by assessing your financial picture in an open-minded fashion can you see where you stand and take control of the situation.*

Note: Be sure to list all assets at their current value without reducing them to reflect any indebtedness. For example, if your home is currently worth $100,000 and you have a $70,000 mortgage, list the house at $100,000 in the asset section; show the $70,000 mortgage in the liability section that follows.

Later in the book we'll look at the various categories of assets; we'll separate them into long-, medium-, and short-term categories; and we'll consider which of these assets appreciate the most reliably. For now, let's focus solely on the issue of net worth.

The net worth worksheet has three possible outcomes:

- Assets equal liabilities
- Assets exceed liabilities
- Liabilities exceed assets

The hope, of course, is that your assets exceed your liabilities. This means that you have a net worth. If your assets equal your liabilities, or if your liabilities exceed your assets, your financial position is obviously weaker than it should be. Whatever the outcome, though, it's crucial for you to face it straight on. There's no advantage in denial. Refusing to acknowledge a less than ideal net worth will limit your ability to overcome the obstacles before you.

Analyzing Your Cash Flow

In addition to preparing a statement of assets and liabilities, you also need to look at your expenses and sources of income. This is your *cash flow analysis*. In financial planning, determining your cash flow is extremely important. There are four reasons why. Assessing your income and expenses will:

- Indicate your ability to save
- Let you size up your standard of living

- Indicate if you're living within or beyond your means
- Highlight problem areas

All of these issues affect your ability to do financial planning, but they're especially significant as you proceed to plan for retirement.

Here's an example of why cash flow is so important. Let's say that you're 45 years old. You intend to retire at age 60, and you feel you're ready to start planning for retirement. To start the planning process, however, you should ask yourself a series of questions that identify your options.

- What do I want my retirement to be like?
- What will my sources of income be during retirement?
- What standard of living would I like to enjoy at that time?
- Will I work?
- Do I intend to move, or will I stay in my current residence?
- How will I cover health care expenses?
- What kinds of insurance coverage should I maintain?
- What is my likely life expectancy, and will my resources suffice if I reach or exceed that expected age?

These are among the many questions that will determine how much retirement income you'll need and what assets you'll have to accumulate to provide that income. By implication, you need to look at how your *current* standard of living will influence your *future* standard of living.

One measure of your current standard of living—perhaps the most important measure, too—is the living expenses you now incur and your ability to pay for them. Performing a cash flow analysis will help you with this assessment. To do this cash flow analysis, you must set forth all the various expenditures you incur on a regular or erratic basis, compare those with your income, and by this means define your current standard of living.

In assessing your current expenses, here are three rules to follow:

- Set forth your expenses in categories.
- Be complete.
- Don't guess too low.

Many people approach this exercise simply by recording the numbers more or less off the top of their heads. However, you may prefer to proceed in a more systematic way. You may actually need to track the figures, either historically (perhaps for the past 6 months) or prospectively (perhaps for the next 3 months), to create a good, detailed record of what the expenses really are. Regardless of your method, you can use the following cash flow worksheet to help you organize your data.

CASH FLOW WORKSHEET

INCOME	MONTHLY	ANNUAL
Salary	_____	
Bonuses	_____	
Self-employment income	_____	
Dividends	_____	
Capital gains	_____	
Interest	_____	
Net rents and royalties	_____	
Social Security	_____	
Pension distributions from trusts or partnerships	_____	
Other income	_____	
Total cash available	_____	$_____
Uses of cash		
Home mortgage (or apartment rent)	_____	
Utility payments	_____	
Gas/oil	_____	
Electricity	_____	
Water	_____	
Sewer	_____	
Home maintenance	_____	

CASH FLOW WORKSHEET (continued)

INCOME	MONTHLY	ANNUAL
Property taxes		
Car payments		
Car/commuting expenses		
Maintenance and repairs		
Gas		
Commuting fees/tolls		
Credit card/loan payments		
Insurance premiums		
Life		
Health		
Disability		
Car		
Home		
Liability		
Other		
Income taxes		
Employment taxes		
Clothing		
Child care		
Food		
Medical expenses		
Education		
Vacations		
Entertainment		
Alimony		
Charitable contributions		
Gifts		
Personal items		
Savings/investments		
Vacation fund		
Emergency fund		
Investment fund		
Other		
Other payments		
Total expenses		$(_____)
Net cash inflow/(outflow)		$_____

You may, of course, need to adapt this cash flow record to reflect your particular situation. The main goal here is to note everything that's a regular expense. In addition, however, you should note erratic expenses as well, such as capital expenditures or purely discretionary items such as gifts and vacations. These include spending for:

- A new car
- Other vehicles (boats, campers, etc.)
- Electronic equipment (computer, satellite dish, etc.)
- Home improvements
- A second home

You should factor in these expenses, too, as you analyze your income and expenditures.

In later chapters of the book we'll explore how to refine your understanding of your assets. For now, your main task is to gain a general sense of where your money comes from and where you're spending it.

STEP 2   SET GOALS

Financial planning is by definition a prospective exercise. Since we can't foresee the future, we have to make certain assumptions about what may occur, then plan for contingencies. Here are some of the questions that influence these assumptions:

- How long will you continue to work?
- What will happen with your income—will it remain the same, rise, or fall?
- What will happen with tax rates?
- What investment rates can you reasonably expect?
- What about the rate of inflation?
- How much involvement do you wish to have in managing your investments?

Your answers to these questions will determine how you must respond to plan for your financial future. In later chapters of *Ernst*

& Young's Financial Planning Essentials, we'll examine each of the issues implicit here, and we'll sort through your options for responding to them. Before we do so, however, we should deal with a more immediate, personal issue: What are your financial goals?

The Importance of Setting Goals

Many people find goal-setting a difficult exercise. Here's an exchange similar to what many financial planners have with some of their clients:

> *Financial Planner:* "What are your financial goals for the next 5 to 15 years?"
>
> *Client:* "Well—I don't really have any."
>
> *Financial Planner:* "Do you plan to retire?"
>
> *Client:* "Of course. I'm just not sure when."
>
> *Financial Planner:* "Do you intend to make any major purchases?"
>
> *Client:* "Probably."
>
> *Financial Planner:* "A new car? Maybe a second home?"
>
> At this point, the client may become more specific.
>
> *Client:* "Now that you mention it, I want to have a second home when I'm 55." And as the planner asks more questions, the client's financial goals begin to clarify. "My wife and I purchased a parcel of land in New Mexico, and we plan to build a house on the land and retire there."

Here are some goals typical of what people indicate to financial planners:

- "I'll need to fund my son's postgraduate education."
- "I want to become financially independent by the time I'm 55."
- "I'd like to buy a bass boat next year."
- "I love to travel, so I'd like to take a major trip each year once I've retired."
- "I'd like to quit my present employer and go into business on my own."

- "I want to have a large estate for my children."
- "I want to make significant gifts to charity."

This client's response—and any other response—implies a financial goal. And to meet any financial goal, you have to take action. First, however, you must take steps to determine what your own goals are and—just as important—what your priorities are in achieving them.

How to Identify Your Financial Goals

Most people never take time to identify their financial goals. They either just don't get sufficiently organized, or else they feel safe "winging it" and making financial decisions as each new situation arises. Yet a realistic framework is vital to the process of fulfilling your goals—not just the goals you're aware of, but also those you may not even have identified. To develop a framework of this sort, you should therefore try to define where you want to be, financially speaking, in the future. The worksheet on financial concerns that follows will help to clarify your thinking.

FINANCIAL CONCERNS

_____	To have adequate funds to cover both routine living expenses and foreseeable future needs, including education expenses for my children.
_____	To minimize income taxes.
_____	To be able to retire comfortably.
_____	To increase the assets going to my heirs by utilizing various estate planning techniques.
_____	To accumulate sufficient assets to enable me to increase my standard of living, acquire a business, purchase a vacation home, etc.
_____	To have sufficient funds and insurance coverage in the event of serious illness.
_____	To develop an investment program that will provide a hedge against inflation.
_____	To accumulate a sizable estate to pass on to my heirs.
_____	To enable my family to maintain their standard of living in the event of my death.

Let's look first at relatively general financial concerns. Given your present economic position, rank the items on the financial concerns chart at the bottom of the previous page in order of personal concern, with 1 = most important and 9 = least important.

By answering these questions, you have begun to get a sense of which financial goals are most important to you. Now let's take the goal-setting process a step further. Having clarified some general concerns, you should identify your specific financial objectives.

Using the worksheet on specific financial goals that follows, designate your most important financial objectives. Use 1 for the most important, 2 for the second in importance, and so forth, for each time frame indicated. An important consideration: The ranking for each objective will probably change from one time period to another as your lifestyle and stage of life continue to change.

Comprehensive or Specific Planning?

At this point, you need to decide what you want from the financial planning process. Do you want a comprehensive view of your financial future? Or are you interested only in specific suggestions on specific financial issues? Either alternative is fine; the deciding issue is simply *what best suits your individual needs*. For example, you may be interested only in retirement planning, in assessing your insurance position, in planning to pay for your children's education, or in estate planning. If so, fine. Your strategies and planning should concentrate primarily on these issues. On the other hand, you may want a full financial "checkup" and a prescription that covers all aspects of your financial life. If so, that suggests a different kind of planning process—one that starts with a general assessment of your current position, then proceeds to a more detailed identification of your goals, which leads in turn to creating a comprehensive plan.

There are many ways to achieve both the specific and the more comprehensive kinds of financial planning. Either way, subsequent chapters of this book will be useful as you undertake the process.

Specific Financial Goals

Goals	Short term (0–1 yrs.)	Medium term (1–5 yrs.)	Long term (5–10 yrs.)	Longest term (>10 yrs.)
Education expenses				
Debt reduction		✓		
Buy a house			✓	
Make home improvements			✓	
Buy a car				
Any other large purchases (e.g., boat, plane, art)			✓	
Take a dream vacation			✓	
Income tax minimization			✓	
Change of employment			✓	
Buy a vacation home				
Financial independence				
Adequate retirement income				
Have children				

SPECIFIC FINANCIAL GOALS (continued)

GOALS	SHORT TERM (0–1 YRS.)	MEDIUM TERM (1–5 YRS.)	LONG TERM (5–10 YRS.)	LONGEST TERM (>10 YRS.)
Increase level of charitable giving				
Buy a retirement home				
Adequate disability income		✓		
Provide for survivor in event of my death		✓		
Be protected against inflation				
Take early retirement				
Start a business				
Fund a buy-sell agreement				
Other				
Other				
Other				
Other				

The Advantages of Event-by-Event Planning

Precisely because individuals' needs differ so widely throughout the life cycle, you may, in fact, need to address many financial issues at once. (Someone in middle age may well be concerned with income tax issues *and* investment issues *and* insurance issues *and* college-funding issues *and* estate planning issues *and* retirement planning issues.) In any case, you can use this book to focus on the issues that, given your stage in life, are most important to you. In short, you should focus not so much on your *age* but, rather, on the *events* that have financial significance to your life.

Here are some of the life events likely to have a major impact on your finances:

- Getting married
- Raising a family
- Buying or selling a home
- Funding children's education
- Pursuing a career
- Starting a business
- Getting divorced
- Dealing with aging parents
- Retiring

Given the variety of issues involved in these different life events, you'll find a targeted approach to financial planning more useful than a scattershot approach. By using a specific, focused process, you can assess where you are in life, what the big events are in the near term, and what financial planning issues you can expect at the time of these events.

What each major life event requires you to do is size up its financial impact and then do what's possible to prepare for the consequences. When you start a family, for instance, your biggest concern is probably protecting your spouse and children financially and building in the appropriate safeguards. Regarding your career, the big concern is maximizing your earned income and your participation in retirement plans. With divorce, the big issue is lessening the emotional and financial devastation that can ensue. With retirement, the issues revolve around establishing stable sources of income and sensible estate planning.

The final stage of setting goals, then, is to prioritize the goals that you've identified. Obviously, the short-term goals may well require the most immediate attention. On the other hand, delaying action on long-term goals (such as retirement) may cause you significant problems down the line. And putting off certain goals is potentially catastrophic. (Neglecting to obtain adequate life insurance and disability insurance is a particularly hazardous temptation.) A list of personal financial goals might look something like this:

Short-Term Goals

- Pay off credit card and consumer debt
- Start savings plan
- Set aside cash for a contingency fund equaling 3 months' expenses
- Acquire additional term life insurance
- Acquire individual disability insurance

Medium-Term Goals

- Start college savings plan
- Diversify investment portfolio
- Convert term life insurance policy to cash-value policy
- Contribute maximum to 401(k) plan and IRA plans

Long-Term Goals

- Purchase retirement property
- Retire at age 62
- Maintain preretirement standard of living during retirement

STEP 3   DEVELOP A PLAN

You're now ready to take your goals and develop a plan for achieving them.

Primary Concerns

When developing a plan, keep three primary concerns in mind: *flexibility, liquidity,* and *minimization of taxes.*

Flexibility. It's important to remember that as you develop your plan, the decisions you make aren't carved in stone. Your personal and financial goals can (and often do) change; you need a plan that's flexible enough to change with your circumstances throughout the major and minor life events you experience.

For example, events such as births, deaths, illnesses, and marriage can affect your goals profoundly. Employment changes, inflation, unusually good or bad investment results, and inheritances will also affect your financial circumstances. For these reasons, you should avoid making plans that are rigid or unresponsive to change.

Liquidity. Similar to the need for flexibility (and closely related to it) is the need to provide for adequate liquidity. Liquidity is, of course, especially important so that you can deal with financial emergencies. Most financial advisors recommend that you have funds available that are equivalent to 3 to 6 months of your expenses. Appropriate locations for these funds are checking, savings, and money market accounts. Other advisors suggest having a standby line of credit to accomplish this same result. The important factor either way is to have sufficient reserves set aside so that you can deal with emergencies.

Liquidity: the characteristic of an asset that can be converted readily to cash without loss of principal.

Minimization of Taxes. The third primary concern is minimizing taxes. Minimizing taxes must serve as a means to meet your objectives; it isn't an end in itself. (Or, as some advisors put it, Don't let the tax "tail" wag the financial "dog.") An effective plan will minimize both income taxes and estate taxes. (Tax strategies aren't noted separately throughout this book, but are interwoven through discussions of other financial planning topics.)

CREATING A PLAN

As for the plan itself, you can proceed in one of several different ways. One is to use a financial planning program on your computer. Software of this sort can streamline the process in the long run, although you'll have to invest some time initially to enter the relevant data. Another way to set up your plan is less high-tech but still reliable: Sketch it out on paper. The most important thing is to determine how to meet your goals, then follow through. A simple plan for the short-term goals mentioned above might look as shown below.

SHORT-TERM GOALS

GOAL	ACTION STEPS
1. Pay off credit card debt	Postpone vacation Reduce entertainment expenses Delay purchase of new car Consolidate debt into home equity loan (interest is generally tax-deductible thereby usually making the debt cheaper)
2. Start savings plan	Fund with savings from goal 1 Reduce discretionary spending Arrange for payroll deduction for savings
3. Start contingency fund	Obtain home equity loan fund from curtailed expenses equivalent to 6 months' expenses (ideally) or unsecured line of credit
4. Acquire $100,000 term insurance	Pay for in cash
5. Acquire supplemental disability insurance	Pay for in cash

You should also create a plan for your intermediate- and long-term goals. Here, again, try to stay flexible. If anything, the need for flexibility increases as your time horizon recedes; you'll have less control over distant events. Remember, too, that the most carefully constructed plan will be worthless unless you actually go ahead and implement it. Keep a record of each action step, including when and how it was accomplished. Be patient—implementing your plan can be a time-consuming process. Your personal situation will dictate whether you decide to proceed with or without professional help. Most people will benefit from assistance at some point, at least in implementing their plan. (See the final section of this chapter for guidelines and suggestions on choosing a financial planner.)

STEP 4   KEEP RECORDS SIMPLE

Keeping accurate, detailed records is important for two main reasons. First, keeping records in a regular, orderly fashion simplifies a task that most people dislike but that almost everyone must do: tracking expenses for tax purposes. If you categorize and note your living and business expenses on a regular basis, the burden of longer-term recordkeeping is easier and less frustrating.

Second, keeping good records has the obvious advantage of letting you know how, where, and how fast you're spending your money. You can track cash flow by category and note when you're spending too much or too little on a particular need. Accurate records allow you to notice "red flags" and alert you to pending financial problems.

Both of these aspects of recordkeeping dovetail conveniently with the process of keeping a budget; they provide a system not just for recording your expenditures and income but also for comparing expenditures against what you've actually budgeted. (We'll get to budgets in a moment.) Ideally, this comparison occurs on an ongoing basis, which allows you to make adjustments proactively rather than on an occasional, reactive basis.

Options for Keeping Records

Is there any best way to keep your financial records? Certainly, some ways are fancier or more elaborate than others, but the "best" way is simply the one that you yourself can maintain most consistently and accurately. The range of possible methods is enormous. The simplest method is to keep track of cash receipts, checkbook entries, and credit card statements. At the other extreme, you can use any of the current fairly sophisticated computer programs for personal financial management. The middle ground involves preparing an annual month-by-month budget (based on checks written and charges made), which you then compare to your actual income and expenditures.

None of these methods is difficult to maintain. The computer programs are the easiest options to use in the long run, but they require a fair amount of attention to set up. The various manual methods require ongoing effort but are the quickest and simplest at the beginning. In all instances, the task is simplified by keeping track of your expenses through checks and credit cards. Frequent use of automated teller machines (ATMs) may be counterproductive in this situation; it's simply more difficult to recall what you spent in cash than it is to look at a checkbook record or an itemized credit card statement. (However, using credit cards for this purpose does not mean racking up big credit card balances. Instead, you should charge your expenditures but pay them off at the month's end, thus avoiding interest charges. Alternatively, you could use a charge card that requires you to pay off the charges each month, such as American Express.)

Using the Information

As noted earlier, one of the great benefits of keeping accurate records is that you can be more realistic about how you spend your money. It's harder to kid yourself about your spending habits when the evidence is right before you in black and white. To analyze what you're spending, you should accumulate your data, record them by whatever means you've chosen, then categorize your expenses. (The categories you've already used for your cash flow analysis are appropriate here, too.)

Something you should check at this point is whether your expenditures seem appropriate given your goals and overall financial situation. There are two ways to consider this issue.

Expenditures in Relation to Objective Norms. There are individual differences in how people spend their money; however, normal limits exist for each category of expense. Financial planners use certain objective norms to identify expenditures that may be problematic. These norms are generally expressed as ratios or percentages. If you found, for instance, that rent accounts for 55% of your overall expenditures, something is probably amiss. Similarly, entertainment costs that take up 25% of your budget could also signal a problem.

Expenditures in Relation to Your Goals and Values. Even if your spending patterns appear to be within normal limits, are you using your money in ways that seem right to *you*? Perhaps you feel that you're spending too much on vacations—even if the percentage of your income isn't out of line compared to what others spend. Perhaps postponing the purchase of a new car will allow you to save money you'll need for your children's education. Do you feel that you're spending too much money *in general*?

On the other hand, you may sense that you're overly stringent with your spending. One example is maintaining an older automobile whose frequent breakdowns inconvenience you or even put you in physical danger; buying a new, more reliable car may serve you well in this instance.

One way or the other, it's quite possible that you should pay more attention to what your hunches are telling you—either to curtail or to increase expenditures. The crux of the matter is that this is your money; you should feel comfortable with how you're using it.

STEP 5	MAKE AN INFORMAL BUDGET

By now you've assessed your financial situation. You've set some goals. You've started keeping detailed records to track your expenses. Now what?

The answer to that question depends largely on what your recordkeeping reveals. You may find yourself in a position where your expenditures clearly exceed your income. You can't realistically do any long-term financial planning until you get out of debt. In this situation, you may decide that more of your income should go toward debt liquidation until you've eliminated most or all of your outstanding debts.

On the other hand, you may find that your income exceeds your expenditures and that your expenditures themselves are within normal limits. In this case, it makes sense for you to invest the excess rather than just park your funds in a low-interest checking account. You can now proceed to start analyzing your risk tolerance and other aspects of the investment process. (We discuss investment planning in detail in upcoming chapters.)

Either way, the whole idea is to gain control over your finances. You want to know what you're spending and why you're spending it, and you want to maintain this knowledge on a continuous basis. The means to this end is making (and following) a budget—a step that goes to the heart of the financial planning process.

The Foundation to Your Budget

It's important to note, however, that several bedrock assumptions should underlie your budget. These assumptions are essentially the foundation that your budget is built upon, and most of them have to do with income:

- Is your job secure?
- Are your other sources of income secure?
- What degree of financial risk are you assuming?

If your job isn't secure, for instance, you may need to set aside more abundant savings and spend less, just in case you end up unemployed. This will give you some funds to tide you over until you find another job. Similarly, your tolerance to financial risk will influence how you budget funds for investments. However, it's important for you to assess these issues as carefully as possible. Wishful thinking has doomed more than a few budgets at the outset.

Setting Up and Following a Budget

Initially, your budget bears a close resemblance to the cash flow analysis you performed earlier. The difference is that the budget isn't a historical record of *what you've spent* but a benchmark for *what you plan to spend*. And in this sense, the budget is a changeable, relatively fluid document. Finding realistic guidelines may require several months' effort before you "get it right."

If you're just starting to keep a budget, you should work at it consistently and you should be conservative in the assumptions you make and in the actions you take. Don't assume more income or fewer expenses just because an optimistic scenario seems likely. Defer whatever gratification you can until you have your guidelines established and can predict accurately what you're bringing in and what you're spending. Don't make big financial commitments at first—these expenditures could be disastrous if your income doesn't reach certain levels. (Commitments of this sort include buying a home or making major investments.) Perhaps you should live more modestly at the beginning. As you establish yourself, however, you can take greater risks.

How should you implement your budget? Generally speaking, you should work from what you've already accomplished—your records of income and expenses—using the method you've already employed. We've already discussed both the high-tech computer method and the low-tech paper-and-pencil method. Both work well. What you must do either way is to use your budget as a way of shaping (and generally that means *limiting*) present and future expenditures. This means having the budget influence your decisions on an ongoing basis.

Using the computer method means inputting your expenditures frequently and in detail—perhaps even day by day—so that you can sense the drift of your overall or specific expenditures. Most financial planning software programs will generate reports about any expense criteria you select. Keeping tabs on your expenditures creates an awareness of how much money remains within a given budget category for that particular month.

The low-tech budget method is predictably more basic but can serve the same end. You post a copy of your budget somewhere you find convenient—next to your kitchen calendar, perhaps, or in your study. You then note your day-by-day expenditures on blank spaces provided next to each expense category. The figures you note serve to remind you of how much remains for each month's expenditures.

Either way, the keys to success for keeping close to budget are:

- Accuracy of recordkeeping
- Consistency of effort
- Discipline in curtailing expenditures

Even the best-designed budget is worthless if you ignore it.

 ## STEP 6 DEAL WITH SHORTFALLS, CREDIT, AND DEBT

If you find that your expenditures exceed your income—or even if the situation seems headed in that direction—you must take immediate action. Otherwise, you're headed for trouble.

The Various Categories of Debt

It's important to look not only at the level of debt you have, but also at the *categories* of debt. Lumping all your debts into one category isn't a useful practice. For instance, lumping home mortgage debt with investment-related debt and personal debt doesn't give you an accurate picture. The interest on home mortgage debt is generally tax-deductible; interest on investment debt may be partially or entirely tax-deductible; interest on most personal debt isn't tax-deductible at all (an exception is some or all of the interest on student loans). The overall implications are fairly straightforward: Home mortgage debt costs less than personal debt. So you should put your debt into those three categories:

- Home mortgage debt
- Investment debt
- Personal debt

If you have personal debt, you should determine why you have it and the degree to which it's necessary. An example: Let's say that you have a car loan following the purchase of a second car. What purpose does this car serve? If you've purchased the car because it's necessary for your work, the debt is probably appropriate. If, however, you've purchased the car simply on whim—and if your overall financial situation doesn't really have room for such a luxury—you should reconsider the wisdom of carrying that debt. It's also important to look at these aspects of debt:

- The level of debt
- The interest rate you're paying
- Whether you can liquidate it in the near future

Problematic Debt

Next we look at some of the most common sources of debt that cause frequent problems.

Credit Cards. Many people get into debt because they overuse their credit cards. Paying with plastic is so easy that one thing leads to another, and soon you've racked up a huge balance. Even with interest rates at "only" 13%, 14%, or 15%, you're paying exorbitantly for what you've purchased.

A habit of paying no more than the minimum monthly payment for your credit card debt compounds the problem. You may feel that you're digging your way out bit by bit, but you're mistaken. In fact, paying only the minimum monthly payment will leave you in debt seemingly forever.

Car Purchases. Like credit cards, car loans are easy to obtain but costly to pay off. Car loan rates may seem reasonable, yet the long-term costs can add up alarmingly. The low rates that many car dealers advertise—2%, even 0%—are often simply a ruse; dealers absorb the costs of offering low interest rates by raising sticker prices.

Impulsive or Compulsive Spending. Of course, one of the main reasons for high levels of debt is simply spending too much. We're all bombarded by incessant advertisements to buy this, that, and whatever. Small wonder that we often succumb to impulse. The sad truth remains: A series of relatively insignificant impulse purchases can add up to enough that you must forgo the funding of more critical financial objectives.

Compulsive spending is even more problematic—an emotional disorder akin to compulsive gambling that warrants professional help.

■ **Tip:** Have a problem with unmanageable debt or compulsive spending? Lots of people do—and many of them are people who may outwardly seem financially high and dry. An organization founded to help people with debt or spending problems is Debtors Anonymous. Modeled after the 12-step Alcoholics Anonymous program, Debtors Anonymous works with people from all backgrounds and socioeconomic levels. For information, check your local phone listings, or write to DA's national headquarters at Debtors Anonymous, P.O. Box 400, Grand Central Station, New York, NY 10163-0400 (www.debtorsanonymous.org). ■

"Keeping Up with the Joneses." Similarly, social pressures to maintain appearances can seem harmless in the short term yet do real damage to your financial health. Whether it's a question of redecorating an already attractive house, dressing in all the latest fashions, or generally living beyond your means, you may well have to resist the external pressures of consumer society to achieve your long-term financial goals.

Ignoring Your Own Financial Goals. And that brings us back to the central issue. What, exactly, are your financial goals? If you've defined them, focusing on them will make the task of avoiding and reducing debt much easier. If you have yet to define them, it's harder to see individual expenditures in the wider context. Ignoring your financial goals can easily result in accumulating unneeded debt.

How to Reduce Debt

Let's say you've concluded that you have too much debt, and you've resolved to reduce it. What are your options? Here are some suggestions.

Reduce Expenditures

This may seem self-evident, but many people avoid facing reality and refuse to cut their level of expenditures. Do you really need to maintain as high a standard of living as you currently have? Is it possible that some of your "needs" are really "wants" instead? Can you find places to trim expenditures even on items that are necessities? Would moving into less expensive housing, for example, ease the financial pressures in other areas of your life? Are there other changes that might cut costs as well or better? Typical categories that warrant scrutiny (or that can tolerate reductions in what you spend) are:

- Entertainment
- Travel
- Clothes
- Gifts
- New cars
- Home improvements

Curtailing credit card expenditures is especially important given the high cost of this kind of debt.

Pay Off Credit Card Debt

The next step is to pay off your credit card debt. Eliminating this kind of debt does more than just take a heavy burden off your finances; it's actually equivalent to earning a significant investment return. For instance, if you pay off a credit card balance that racks up interest at a 15% rate, liquidating that debt is like earning 15% on an investment.

(Paying off that debt would, of course, be an important step to take before investing your money in ways that offer lower yields. If you invest money at 7% while paying 15% to service debt, you're still losing the 8% difference between your debt and the investment. Tolerating that level of loss doesn't make sense. Pay off the debt first.)

If you're able to pay off your credit card debt only over the long haul, consider doubling up payments to diminish the monthly service charges. The faster you pay off the debt, the lower your overall cost.

Consolidate or Transfer Debt

If you can't eliminate the debt altogether, you might consolidate your debts or transfer some or all of them to another creditor. This course of action won't eliminate debt, but it can make it cheaper. Here are some alternatives:

Find a cheaper credit card. Obtain credit with a company offering a lower-rate card, then pay off the expensive debt with the cheaper debt. For a current list of low-interest credit cards, contact Bankcard Holders of America, 560 Herndon Parkway, Suite 120, Herndon, VA 22070. This nonprofit organization charges a $4.00 fee for the information.

Obtain a home equity loan. This arrangement allows you to pay off the high-rate credit card debt, then service the lower-rate, tax-deductible loan at a considerable savings. One risk here: Home equity loans have specific, rigid contractual terms which, if violated, can put your home ownership in jeopardy.

Get help from a nonprofit agency. Many cities and some states have agencies that will help you analyze your debt problems, consolidate debt, and negotiate with creditors to arrange a repayment schedule.

Switch to Debit Cards

Since credit cards often lead to excessive and expensive debt, you might try debit cards as an alternative. Debit cards work much like an ATM card: Every debit you make is deducted from your checking account. The difference—and convenience—is that you can use a debit card not only at automated teller machines but at a growing variety of retailers. The advantages are obvious. Although a debit card won't stop you from spending, it will certainly prevent you from spending money that isn't in your account. The awareness of your balance can serve as a restraint. Unfortunately, your own bank may not offer debit card services; you may need to switch banks to obtain one.

Use Savings to Pay Off Debt

You can also tap your savings to liquidate debt. The disadvantage of this course of action is obviously that it diminishes your savings; the advantage, however, is that you will get out from under the burden of long-term debt. Take care, of course, that using your savings doesn't leave you vulnerable to unanticipated expenses or a temporary loss of income.

Borrow from Your Family

Hitting up your relatives for a loan may sound simplistic, but it's worth considering. It's certainly a time-honored method for temporarily easing a debt crunch. Although not without risks—chiefly in the potential strain on relationships—this method can be an important alternative.

Borrowing from your family doesn't necessarily mean that you borrow interest-free. You might, for instance, offer to pay interest at a level that splits the difference between an interest-free loan and the loan you're trying to liquidate. (If you were paying off a credit card balance calculated at a 14% rate, the interest rate on the loan from your relative would be 7%.) This would offer advantages to all parties involved. You'd cut the cost of debt in half, and your relative would earn an interest rate considerably higher than that in most current liquid accounts. No matter what terms you arrange, however, you should put the agreement in writing and make sure that everyone understands the terms.

File for Bankruptcy. As a last resort, you can declare bankruptcy. *This is a major calculated gamble.* Bankruptcy is not to be taken lightly. You should seek legal and financial counseling before taking this step. On the one hand, declaring bankruptcy eliminates some of your current debts; on the other hand, bankruptcy inflicts 7 years of damage to your credit rating. It's important to note, as well, that *declaring bankruptcy absolves you only from certain debts*, among them:

- Credit card debt
- Medical bills
- Auto loans
- Utility bills
- Rent

It does not allow you to cancel other debts, including:

- Child support
- Alimony payments
- Student loans
- Taxes (some very old tax liabilities may be discharged)
- Court-ordered damages

If you're on the verge of bankruptcy, you can take a series of steps to protect yourself, to deal with your creditors, and to set forth a clear, rational plan for liquidating the debt.

The Income Side

On the other hand, perhaps the credit and debt problems you face aren't limited to spending too much; perhaps you're simply not earning what you need to maintain the standard of living you desire. Under these circumstances, what can you do to increase your income? Here are two possibilities that may make a difference in this regard.

First, if you're working 9 to 5, you might consider other employment in addition to your regular job—a temporary arrangement, perhaps, that will get you through your current hard times. Such an arrangement might allow you to pay off your debt, thus putting you in a more favorable position.

A second possibility is to lower your standard of living temporarily to finance the costs of reeducating yourself or your spouse. Perhaps further education will allow you to pursue a career conducive to the living standard you want. Education is expensive; however, it's one of the best investments that you can make—both financially and in many nonfinancial ways.

STEP 7 REVIEW YOUR PROGRESS

How often you review your financial plan depends on how old you are, what kind of planning you've decided to do, and what life event you're planning for. In most cases, an annual review of your financial plan is adequate. If you've just begun the process, however, or if you have some significant financial problems, a more frequent review is probably appropriate. Many people find a monthly review helpful. When problems are severe, even a weekly review may be advisable. But in most cases, an annual update will serve your purposes.

Here are the general questions to ask:

- Have your financial goals stayed the same?
- Are you meeting your budget?
- Are you earning the investment rates of return you anticipated?
- To what degree is inflation affecting your finances?
- Has your tax situation changed?

By answering these questions, you can decide whether your financial assumptions have been correct and whether your overall situation has changed.

Do You Need a Financial Planner?

Although this book and other resources may serve you well in planning your financial future, no single source of printed information can answer all readers' questions. Even computer programs and other interactive media are subject to inherent constraints in providing data and advice. For this reason, you may end up choosing to consult a financial planner at some point for specific, personalized counsel on one or more aspects of your individual situation.

When, exactly, should you seek help from a financial planner? That question has no single answer. One determining factor is your level of income. If you're making $30,000 a year, for example, you probably won't need a financial planner under most circumstances. If, however, you've earned $30,000 a year and now find yourself on the verge of bankruptcy, you may well benefit from a professional planner's financial advice. (Unfortunately, one complicating factor is that a financial planner's fees may aggravate your money problems still further.) In addition to income level, though, the issues that prompt many people to seek help from a financial planner are issues of complexity. This is particularly true when you get into such areas as estate planning, tax planning, and retirement planning.

When to Seek Help

Next we outline the three main reasons for you to consult a financial planner.

Confirmation. Let's say that you're capable of setting your own financial course, and you do a good job of it. However, you want the sense of confirmation that a professional can provide. A financial planner can check your numbers, review your goals, suggest alternative courses for attaining them, and provide a "second opinion" on your plan's fundamental soundness.

More Detailed Guidance. On the other hand, perhaps you find financial planning difficult even when you have an overall sense of direction. You may feel intimidated by quantitative analyses or overwhelmed by the numerous investment options available. Despite having the books and software programs to help you do your own planning, you don't feel confident of how to proceed. Or else you've taken the initial steps for do-it-yourself planning, but you now need advice on investment strategies, sophisticated insurance planning, or estate planning. Here, too, a financial planner can provide more detailed guidance.

Financial Planning from the Ground Up. Finally, you may feel sufficiently overwhelmed by the tasks of good financial planning that you decide to seek professional help for comprehensive advice. In such cases you clearly need a financial planner from the start. One caveat, however: *Seeking help on these issues, even on a broad basis, doesn't absolve you from having to make decisions.* It's your money; it's your future. Just as expert legal or medical advice doesn't eliminate the need for you to choose a course of action, expert financial advice leaves you with the fundamental responsibility to chart your course.

If one of these reasons matches your situation, you should consider the possibility of consulting a financial planner. In all three situations, a financial planner can offer some or all of the following kinds of help:

- Identifying problems and goals
- Identifying strategies for reaching your goals
- Setting priorities
- Providing advice on tax issues
- Saving you time on research
- Purchasing commission-free financial products
- Providing objectivity
- Helping you with specific finance-related tasks

Options for Financial Planning

There are two main categories of financial planners: commission-based and fee-based. (A third category of planners—those who charge you both a fee and some commission as well—are somewhat less common than the other two.)

Commission-Based Planner. Commission-based planners provide financial advice; then, in the late stages of the planning process, they sell you products to meet the needs you've identified—needs for insurance, investment products, and so forth. You pay for these services through commissions on whatever products you purchase. The chief advantage of this arrangement is that it provides one-stop shopping. The chief disadvantage is that basing the planner's fee on commissions may prompt questions about his or her objectivity and independence. In some instances, you may have to look elsewhere to obtain products unavailable through the commission-based planner. You can find commission-based financial planners at brokerage houses, insurance companies, and financial planning boutiques.

Fee-Based Planner. By contrast, fee-based financial planners provide advice but not the actual products themselves. The arrangement is strictly fee for service. There are no commissions. The advantage of this arrangement is a more predictable degree of objectivity and independence, since the fee-based planners have no vested interest in one product over another. The disadvantage is that you pay the fee outright, regardless of whether you act on the advice or not; the cost of any commissions on investments, insurance, and so forth, is in addition to the advisory fee. The biggest players of this sort are accounting firms, accompanied by some fee-only boutique planning firms.

Sizing Up Financial Planners

How do you know if the financial planner you've selected is qualified and responsive to your individual needs? Unfortunately, it's sometimes hard to know in advance; choosing carefully in the first place is your best safeguard. One way to hedge your bets is to start by considering planners who are accredited by one or more of the standard professional organizations. The most common credentials are described below.

Personal Financial Specialist (PFS). These planners are CPAs who have taken the additional steps of preparing for and passing a rigorous, comprehensive financial planning exam administered by the American Institute of Certified Public Accountants. They must also receive recommendations from their clients and from other financial advisors, and have a minimum of 3 years' financial planning experience, including a minimum of 500 hours per year in financial planning.

Certified Financial Planner (CFP). Planners with the CFP credential may have taken courses and have passed six exams administered by the Institute of Certified Financial Planners. They have at least 3 years of work experience, and have a continuing education requirement each year.

Chartered Financial Consultant (ChFC). The ChFC credential results from a 10-course sequence during a 2- to 4-year period of study; 2-hour exams are required at the conclusion of each course.

Masters of Science in Financial Services (MSFS). The MSFS credential follows 40 hours of coursework and a 2-week residency at the American College in Bryn Mawr, Pennsylvania (which also grants the Chartered Financial Consultant credential).

Registered Financial Planner (RFP). The International Association of Registered Financial Planners grants the RFP credential following completion of academic and practical requirements.

In addition to selecting someone with proper credentials, you should also consider the following aspects of financial planners' backgrounds.

Experience. How long has the planner worked for clients with your needs? Even the most heavily credentialed planner should have at least a few years' experience in the field pertinent to your questions. Some planners specialize. Is your planner's specialty in keeping with your needs? A specialist in investments may not serve you best if your concern is estate planning.

Access to Experts. In a complex and fast-changing field, no one can maintain complete knowledge of all aspects of personal finance. A planner should therefore be willing and able to consult with colleagues on matters affecting your financial future.

Fees and Commissions. As in other fields, fees for financial planning vary. You should clarify in advance what services you will receive and what fees or commissions will be charged. Consider the possibility of shopping around; although the time involved may seem burdensome at first, you may find considerable disparity among several planners.

Here are some situations that might warrant concern as you select and work with a financial planner:

- Does the financial plan you receive have a "canned" feel to it?
- Do all the planner's recommendations involve buying products that the planner's own company sponsors?
- Has the planner been in business for just a short while?

Finally, keep in mind that even if you end up hiring a helpful, thoughtful, experienced financial planner, the arrangement doesn't absolve you from responsibility. You still have to do your homework. You still end up making the ultimate decisions. The financial planner will offer recommendations and advice, not a free ride to painless or anxiety-free wealth.

2

BUILDING WEALTH TO MEET YOUR GOALS

Now that you've gained an overview of the financial planning process, let's turn to the first of its three main disciplines: building wealth. For no matter what your goals—funding your children's education, raising your standard of living, saving for retirement—building wealth is one of the fundamental ways that will help you reach your financial destination.

In this chapter and the four that follow we explain the many ways in which you can build wealth. Most of these chapters concern investment planning. Before we delve into the complexities of that subject, however, let's consider the importance of retirement plans and savings.

BUILDING WEALTH THROUGH RETIREMENT PLANS

One of the best ways to build wealth is by participating in retirement plans. These plans encourage you to save both because they provide a disciplined approach to saving and because they all provide tax advantages. Among the tax advantages: The contributions and investment returns are not taxed until they are distributed to you.

Company Plans

Most company retirement plans are *qualified plans*.

> **Qualified plan:** *a plan that meets certain requirements that enable it to offer tax advantages to both the company and the employees.*

The most common kinds of qualified plans are:

- Pension plans
- Profit-sharing plans
- Employee stock ownership plans (ESOPs)
- 401(k) and 403(b) plans

Pension Plans. Pension plans have been the most traditional form of corporate retirement plans: In recent years, however, some companies have been moving away from retirement planning arrangements of this type.

For the most part, employer pension plans (also called *defined benefit plans*) are a relatively painless way to build wealth for retirement. Under a pension plan, when you retire you receive a monthly pension benefit determined by the plan's formula. Pension plans provide the greatest benefit for you when you work for a particular company over the long haul—for 25 or 30 years, for example.

If you're working for a company that provides a pension benefit, you should consider the benefit that you will forgo before changing jobs. The salary and benefits you would accrue from a new job must be high enough to compensate you for the additional pension benefits you would earn if you stayed put.

Here's an example. Assume that you work 10 years at Company A, then switch to Company B and work there 10 years also. Assume as well that both companies have the same pension plan and that your salary is $30,000 and growing at 5% per year. Look at how large the difference in your annual retirement benefit could be if you stayed with Company A for 20 years compared to switching to Company B.

	YEARS WORKED	PENSION BENEFIT
Company A	10	$ 7,053
Company B	10	11,490
		$18,543
Company A	20	$22,980
Company B	0	0
		$22,980

The difference of $4,437 per year occurs because the benefit is computed according to your salary level prior to termination and your years of service with the employer.

Profit-Sharing Plans. Rather than providing a pension plan, some companies have adopted a profit-sharing plan (also called a *defined contribution plan*). Your company determines its total contribution. One variable here is how well your company does during a particular year. A rise or drop in profits can create a proportional increase or decrease in the amount contributed to the plan. Another variable is how well the investments of the plan perform. At retirement, you receive payments that are equal to your allocable share of the plan investments.

Employee Stock Ownership Plans (ESOPs). ESOPs also allow you to share in your company's success. An ESOP is a qualified plan that invests primarily in the securities of the employer.

Contributions to the plan are not primarily dependent on the employer's profits. Like a profit-sharing plan, an ESOP provides a formula for allocating the contributions among the participants. You have the potential of gaining from such an investment in your company if the company stock value increases over time. If the plan invests only in your own company's stock, however, changes in the value of that stock will affect your account value.

401(k) and 403(b) Plans. Increasingly popular during the past few years, 401(k) plans are tax-deferred retirement plans that provide unusual flexibility. These plans allow you to set aside a portion of your salary on a before-tax basis and then have these funds invested in the plan for your retirement; however, certain restrictions apply to your before-tax contributions. (See *The Ernst & Young Tax Guide*, annually published by John Wiley & Sons, Inc., for more details.)

An added benefit is that your employer may match your contribution to some degree. In situations that include your employer's contribution, you have especially strong reasons to save for retirement by this means. Your employer's contribution is essentially a kind of raise—one you can't spend until retirement—but your only option for receiving it is by contributing to the plan. Then, when you retire, you receive the combined contributions, plus whatever the investment has earned.

Often, 401(k)s have specific advantageous features, including:

- *Loan provisions*
- *Flexible investment options*
- *Employer matching contributions*

E X A M P L E ■ Janice needed to buy a new car. Instead of taking out a standard auto loan from a bank, however, she borrowed the money from her 401(k) plan. The rules stipulated that she take out a 5-year loan; the length of this term suited her purposes as well as meeting the requirements. Janice then paid off the loan in monthly installments, just as she would have paid off a bank loan—except that she was essentially paying the interest to *herself* instead. ■

A 401(k) plan encourages you to save for three main reasons:

- Automatic payroll deductions make saving easy.
- Company contributions, if any, apply only if you contribute to the plan.
- Tax law and plan distribution provisions encourage you to keep your money invested.

A 403(b) plan is a type of retirement plan sponsored by certain religious, charitable, and public educational organizations. Like a 401(k) plan, it allows employees of these organizations to set aside part of their compensation and have the funds invested for their retirement.

If you're eligible to contribute to a 401(k) or 403(b) plan, doing so is a definite "must" because of their distinct tax advantages. The only common disadvantage is that the asset isn't easily available for you to spend until after your retirement. However, this may prove an advantage, since it encourages you to save for retirement. Normally 401(k) and 403(b) plans are considered very good savings options due to their ability to defer taxes on some of your salary and investment income.

Other Retirement Plans

In addition to the plans we've discussed, here are other kinds of retirement plans to consider:

- Individual Retirement Accounts
- Keoghs and SEPs

Individual Retirement Accounts (IRAs). IRAs allow you a maximum annual contribution of $2,000 as long as you have earned income of that amount. Married couples in which one spouse does not have any earnings are permitted to make contributions of $4,000 per year as long as no more than $2,000 per year is deposited in either one of the spouse's IRAs. A single limit applies to all IRA contributions for the year. Your IRA investments then grow tax deferred until you withdraw the money. Withdrawing your money before age 59½ results in a 10% penalty.

(There are a few exceptions to this rule, however.) IRA contributions fall into two categories: *deductible* and *nondeductible*. Since 1986, only people who aren't participating in a company retirement plan, or who are and whose adjusted gross income falls below certain limits, can deduct their contributions. (See the IRA deductions table below.) Even if your IRA contribution is nondeductible, contributing to the account may make good sense—assuming, of course, that you feel confident that you won't need the money before the 59½ minimum age for withdrawal without penalty—and you should start contributing as soon as you can.

Starting in 1998 a new kind of IRA—the Roth IRA—is available. Contributions to a Roth IRA are nondeductible, but if you meet certain requirements the income you earn in the Roth IRA will be tax *free* when you withdraw it. You can contribute to a Roth IRA even if you're over 70½ and you can convert your regular IRA into a Roth IRA. Income from a Roth IRA will be tax free if you've had it for 5 years and the payments are made after you reach age 59½, die, or are disabled, or for up to $10,000 for a first-time home purchase.

If you are not eligible to make a deductible IRA contribution you will always be better off making a Roth IRA contribution instead of a nondeductible IRA contribution. Your ability to make a Roth IRA contribution is limited by your income; if your adjusted gross income is more than $110,000 (single) or $160,000 (married, filing jointly) you cannot make a Roth IRA contribution. The contribution is phased out between $95,000 and $110,000 (single) or $150,000 to $160,000 (married, filing jointly).

E
X
A
M
P
L
E

■ Compare the value of IRAs at age 65 under two scenarios: Suppose that Leonore and Janice are the same age. Leonore contributed $2,000 per year to her IRA starting at age 35. Janice also contributed $2,000 per year, but she started when she was 45. Both women earned 8% interest on their IRAs. At the time that they both turned 65, however, Leonore's IRA was worth $244,692, while Janice's was valued at $98,846. ■

IRA Deductions: Adjusted Gross Income (in $) Allowable Deduction			
Married filing jointly[a]	**Single**	**Not an active participant**	**Active participant**
0–49,999	0–29,999	2,000	2,000
50,000–58,999	30,000–38,999	2,000	200–2,000[b]
59,000–59,999	39,000–39,999	2,000	200[c]
60,000 and over	40,000 and over	2,000	0

[a] A married couple filing separately is subject to a special limitation
[b] The $2,000 amount is reduced by a percentage equal to your adjusted gross income in excess of the lower adjusted gross income limits divided by $10,000. For example, a single person with an adjusted gross income of $32,000 is allowed an IRA deduction of $1600.
[c] The IRA deduction will not be reduced below $200 until it is reduced to $0 at $60,000 (married filing jointly) and $40,000 (single) of adjusted gross income.
NOTE: The amounts shown above are for 1998. The AGI limits change each year until 2007.

You can convert your regular IRA into a Roth IRA if your AGI is not more than $100,000. You must include the value of your regular IRA in income but, if you convert before 1999, you can spread the inclusion over 4 years.

Setting up an IRA is simple if you follow these suggestions:

First, *decide on the investment vehicle you prefer.* There are rules regarding what you can and cannot invest in, but you have considerable leeway to choose from most of the available vehicles. (A sample exception: You can't invest in life insurance inside an IRA.)

Second, establish your IRA through a bank, insurance company, brokerage firm, or mutual fund company that offers numerous appropriate investment choices.

Third, make your IRA contribution as early as possible each year and no later than April 15 of the following year.

Keoghs, SEPs, and SIMPLEs. A Keogh plan is a retirement plan that is available to anyone who has self-employment income. This is generally income from any unincorporated business that you conduct. A simplified employee pension (SEP) is a plan that allows an employer to make contributions toward an employee's retirement without becoming involved in more complex retirement plans. If you are self-employed, you can contribute to your own SEP.

Even if your employer makes contributions to a SEP for your account, you can make contributions to your own IRA. The IRA deduction rules discussed previously apply to any amounts you contribute to your IRA.

A SIMPLE (Savings Incentive Match Plan for Employees) allows small employers to set up a plan where employees can contribute on a pretax basis without having to deal with complicated discrimination rules.

10 Big Mistakes in Investing — #1
Buying tax-favored investments (e.g., municipal bonds, Series EE bonds) inside tax-advantaged vehicles (i.e., IRAs, Keoghs)

For instance, on municipal bonds you pay no federal or state income tax if the bonds are issued by the state in which you live or by a municipality in that state. If, however, you put such a financial instrument into your tax-deferred retirement account, the income earned becomes taxable when you receive the money from the plan. In effect, you have converted a tax-free investment into a low earning, taxable one. Series EE U.S. Savings Bonds are taxed at the federal level, but generally only when you redeem them so there is no benefit from putting them into the plan. Also, the income is not subject to state income tax. Again, by putting them into a tax-deferred retirement account, you subject them to tax at the time you take disbursements from your fund.

BUILDING WEALTH THROUGH SAVINGS

Saving money is one of those things that almost everyone considers a good idea but too few people actually do to a large enough degree. We all have our reasons: not enough income, too many bills, no time to check out the available savings plans. Unfortunately, the need to save will haunt you even if you stall for time. Unless you inherit a fortune, win the lottery, or simply earn so much money that you have all you'll ever need, you simply won't succeed at building wealth unless you save.

One rule of thumb is that you should save at least 10% of your annual gross income toward your retirement goal. If you're past 50 and still haven't started saving toward retirement, the figure for necessary savings will rise to 20%.

Most people find this "savings bite" painful. It *is* painful. Still, it's generally less painful than the alternatives, most of which involve eventually running short of the money you need in order to do important things—whether that means retiring comfortably, educating your kids, starting a business, or having a contingency fund sufficient to protect you during unemployment or other setbacks.

What compensates for the pain of saving is the payoff from *compounding*. This is a relatively straightforward mathematical process by which your money increases in value, slowly at first, then with much more dramatic speed. The following table illustrates the power of compounding for a saver depositing $300 a month.

COMPOUNDING TABLE FOR SAVER DEPOSITING $300 A MONTH					
After-Tax Return	Year 5	Year 10	Year 15	Year 20	Year 25
4%	$19,890	$44,175	$ 73,827	$110,032	$154,239
5%	20,402	46,585	80,187	123,310	178,653
6%	20,931	49,164	87,246	138,612	207,898
7%	21,478	51,925	95,089	156,278	243,022
8%	22,043	54,884	103,811	176,706	285,308
9%	22,627	58,054	113,522	200,366	336,337

Saving well means saving regularly enough—and, ideally, *early* enough—so that your money has plenty of time to compound. For most people, this means having more than just the *desire* to save.

Setting Up a Savings Plan

The key to building wealth successfully through savings is to have a plan. There are many ways to accomplish this goal, but here's a method that many people find useful.

STEP 1 | Start as Soon as Possible

Don't wait until some ideal time to start your savings plan. No time will seem ideal; you'll always find excuses to delay another month. At some point you simply have to take the plunge. The earlier you start, the better "grip" you'll have on your finances.

STEP 2 | Forecast Your Cash Flow

You should forecast your anticipated cash flow for various increments of the year. Usually, this means forecasting the year on a monthly basis. Once you determine your income and expenses, how much is left over?

STEP 3 | Project Monthly Savings

Start with anticipated monthly savings; then project for the entire year. This may involve averaging. For instance, if you can save $330 in February and $270 in March, you might decide to save $300 a month.

STEP 4 | Pay Yourself First

What this means is that on receiving your monthly salary, the very first check you write is the $300 payment for your savings. Alternatively, you may be able to arrange for an automatic payroll deduction at your workplace, or arrange for automatic monthly or weekly transfers from your checking account to your investment account.

STEP 5	## CONTRIBUTE MORE WHENEVER POSSIBLE

The $300 monthly savings amount shouldn't be where you stop; it's just the start. If, for instance, you receive bonuses as part of your compensation (or if you receive some sort of windfall, such as an inheritance), you should consider contributing part or all of it to your savings plan. The extra money may seem an opportunity to enhance your current lifestyle; on the other hand, it's also a great opportunity to enhance your future lifestyle.

STEP 6	## REVIEW YOUR PLAN AT THE SAME TIME EACH YEAR

Consistent annual review is important to maintaining an effective savings plan. Any time you choose can serve the purpose; however, you might pick the time of year during which you find out what your annual raise will be. Undertaking your review at that time will help you plan how to use your increased cash flow most productively.

PLANNER Don't be surprised if you wind up unable to save the amount that your savings plan specifies. Most people's actual expenses exceed what they've anticipated—there are always unexpected costs!

Here are some do's and don'ts to help you save:

Don't just sit down at the kitchen table with pen and paper and try to guess your expenses. Pull out the check register from your checkbook and gather your credit card receipts for the last 12 months. Total your *actual* expenses. Study them. See what the patterns are. You'll probably find that your living expenses are a lot higher than you thought.

Do write your check to your savings before you write any other check that month. However, make sure to deposit that check in an investment that's liquid—just in case you need to pull some money back out by month's end.

Don't get frustrated if your savings plan specifies $300 per month but you've only saved $100 monthly during the last 6 months. You may need a year or so to determine how much you can really save each month.

Do start now—even if you can only save $10. Ten dollars per month growing at 8% per year equals $35,143 in 40 years.

Finding the Right Balance

A successful savings plan obviously depends on more than just setting up a plan. It's no secret that success over the long haul requires both the discipline to save and a positive view of saving. Discipline should be self-evident: The more consistently you save, the more reliably the money will add up. A positive view of saving means that you feel fundamentally right about setting aside money rather than spending it. However, part of the task of saving goes beyond either factor; it's a question of finding the right balance.

E
X
A
M
P
L
E
■ Samantha and Pete agreed that they ought to start a savings plan. They both felt committed to the task and aware that a degree of belt-tightening would result. After crunching the numbers, Samantha concluded that she and her husband should set aside $300 per month; Pete however, worried that the amount his wife advocated would end up feeling burdensome. He argued that a monthly contribution of $150 or $175 made more sense. The young couple discussed the issue for several

months. Then, seeing their opportunity slip away, they decided to take a more flexible approach. They compromised and chose an initial savings payment of $250 per month. Saving $250 consistently made more sense than saving $300 sporadically. As it turned out, Pete and Samantha managed to reach their goal of saving $300 per month in less than a year's time. ■

You may find the startup phase of saving more difficult than later stages. Once you have a savings mechanism in place, however, it will force you to start looking at your expenses and seeing more clearly what's crucial and what isn't. You may find, too, that saving money is easier than you thought. Saving $300 a month may seem easy enough that $350 is an acceptable next step. Soon you'll be saving more than you thought possible.

Other Aspects of Saving

In addition to the steps discussed above, here are three other aspects of saving you may need to consider:

- Setting up a contingency fund
- Saving if you're self-employed
- Saving by paying extra principal on a mortgage

Contingency fund: *a source of liquid assets (usually at least 3 to 6 months' expenses) intended to cover some or all of your expenses during a period of diminished cash flow, unemployment, or personal emergency. Synonyms:* emergency reserve *or* rainy-day fund.

Setting Up a Contingency Fund

Everyone should have a contingency fund. Regardless of whether you're self-employed or on a payroll, you should have sufficient liquid assets available to meet your financial needs during an emergency or disruption of your income. The rule of thumb is that your contingency fund should equal at least 3 months of your expenses. The size of your contingency fund will depend on the nature of your work and the variability of your income. If you're self-employed, you may be more vulnerable to inconsistent cash flow. Even if you have a salaried position, however, the financial ground underfoot may be less solid than you imagine.

Some financial advisors recommend not only a liquid savings account but a second source of emergency funds as well. This source can take the form of credit cards or a line of credit. (Note, however, that you must arrange for a line of credit *before* a personal or professional emergency occurs, since most institutions are unlikely to extend credit if your situation has become precarious.)

Fixed expenses: *personal or business expenses (generally paid monthly or annually) over which you have little or no control. Compare to variable expenses—those costs over which you have some degree of control.*

Saving if You're Self-Employed

If you're self-employed, you'll have fixed and variable expenses that affect your ability to save. Your savings plan under these circumstances will be somewhat more complex than for salaried employees. Everyone has certain expenses that must be covered before he or she can save. For the self-employed person, however, these are generally higher. For this reason, you'll have to do a lot more planning to see what income is coming in and what expenses you must pay. You should also consider accumulating a larger contingency fund than you'd have otherwise, since you have no employer whose benefits—sick days, leave of absence, etc.—serve as a safety net.

Self-employed persons should set up a business contingency fund as well as one for personal needs. The amount should typically equal 6 months of fixed business expenses. The precise amount will depend on the nature of your work and the variability of your income.

10 Big Mistakes in Investing — #2 Failing to maintain a sufficient contingency fund

You may be required to sell a long-term investment (a stock or stock mutual fund, for example) in a down market in order to raise cash.

Saving by Paying Extra Principal on a Mortgage

Some people feel that paying extra principal on their mortgage is a logical and convenient use of funds. However, choosing to make these payments is an investment decision that you should consider carefully.

Generally speaking, you probably don't want to start paying down your mortgage until you have a contingency fund set up, plus ideally some other investments as well. The reason is *liquidity*. During good economic times, paying extra principal may seem to make good sense; during an economic downturn, however, you could end up unemployed and thus need access to liquid assets. A shortage of assets that you can easily turn into cash at such a time could be disastrous. Whatever extra payments you've made on your mortgage contribute to your equity, but that equity isn't readily accessible. By paying down the mortgage quickly you're making a decision not to diversify your investment portfolio. For these reasons, extra payments of principal should generally fall low on a list of savings options. You should build other assets—assets that you can draw on and use to diversify your portfolio—before paying down the mortgage. (See the discussion of diversification in Chapter 4.) Also, remember that paying extra principle reduces the interest you will pay over time, which generally would be tax deductible. If you have a low-interest mortgage, and an opportunity to invest the extra principle payment in an investment with a higher return than the tax-effective rate of your mortgage interest, you should probably do that.

> **Liquidity:** *the characteristic of an asset that can be converted readily to cash without loss of principal.*

Savings Options

Now that you've decided to start saving money, where should you put it? There are all sorts of options—some of which we'll discuss now, some in forthcoming chapters. One consideration you should start to address, however, is tax benefits. Tax-deferred compounding can do wonders for your savings plan. (Note, however, that *for tax reasons, there are strong reasons **not** to withdraw funds from these plans too early*.)

Here are a few tax-advantaged savings vehicles:

401(k) Plans. If available through your employer, your 401(k) plan clearly represents your most attractive savings vehicle. The tax advantages and plan flexibility (such as multiple investment options and loan privileges) are unmatched by any other type of savings vehicle.

If your 401(k) plan includes an employer matching contribution, unless you have cash flow or liquidity problems, you should contribute at least the maximum amount that will be matched by your employer. For example, your company makes a contribution of $1 for every $2 of your salary that you contribute, with a maximum company contribution of 3% of your salary. In this case, you should contribute at least 6% and receive the matching contribution of 3%. The employer's matching contribution is the equivalent of an immediate 50% return on your investment!

Next, and again, unless you have cash flow problems, you should contribute at least the maximum amount that the law allows on a pretax or tax-deferred basis. (The law sets limits as to the total amount that can be contributed to a 401(k) plan.) You will have more dollars working for you than if you had chosen not to make the contribution.

Finally, and again, absent cash flow problems, you should also make the maximum allowable after-tax contributions to the plan. After-tax contributions to a 401(k) plan are like nondeductible contributions to an IRA. In both cases, you do not get a deduction for the contributions. However, unlike nondeductible IRA contributions, your after-tax 401(k) contributions may be available to you currently (albeit with limitations) through the loan provisions of the plan. You can't borrow from an IRA.

IRAs. Before 1986, you could make tax-deductible contributions to an IRA even if you were a participant in an employer retirement plan. As discussed earlier, deductible IRA contributions are now limited if you are a participant in an employer plan, although nondeductible contributions may be allowed. Starting in 1998 you may also be able to contribute to a Roth IRA.

Since 1986, many people have simply stopped making IRA contributions, knowing that their contributions would be non-deductible. These people failed to appreciate the power of tax-deferred compounding. Unless you will need the funds before age 59½ for an identifiable need such as college costs or a major purchase, consider making maximum annual contributions to an IRA. If you're eligible to contribute to a Roth IRA you should definitely consider it.

Keogh, SEP, or SIMPLE. As discussed above, these plans are available to you if you have any type of self-employment income. You may be surprised to learn the types of income that are considered self-employment income. For example, director's fees are self-employment income, as are executor fees if you are a professional executor. And commission income is self-employment income if you are not considered an employee.

Other Investments and Investment Vehicles. A 401(k) plan, an IRA, and a Keogh are all tax-advantaged retirement plans through which you can invest in a wide variety of investments. There are also certain investments which themselves offer tax advantages, including municipal bonds and tax-deferred annuities. Such investments may or may not be appropriate for you. We discuss municipal bonds in detail in Chapter 3 and annuities in Chapter 5.

In Chapter 4 we discuss the most fundamental investment decision that you must make—how much of your capital should you invest or allocate among the major investment categories such as cash, stocks, and bonds? This process is known as asset allocation.

INHERITANCE AND
OTHER UNEXPECTED WINDFALLS

If you receive an inheritance, win the lottery, or gain some other windfall, you will obviously find that your financial options have expanded. You may feel that an unexpected gain should allow you some unexpected pleasures. But you could save the extra money. Consider investing the after-tax proceeds so that you can retire early and live better in the future. Alternatively, you could help out some of your family members or give something back to your community. If you make a donation to charity, you may not only contribute to a worthy cause but also benefit from a tax standpoint, given the possibility of a charitable deduction. The important thing is to consider your alternatives and plan carefully. It's nice to get a reward or windfall, but it's also useful to consider how the extra cash can pay off in the long run.

Regarding inheritance: To the degree possible, you should try to coordinate your estate plan with your parents' (or with anyone from whom you know you will be inheriting money). Many options exist that can save your family money and heartache as each generation considers what it will provide for the next generation. See Chapters 9 to 13 on estate planning to explore these issues in detail.

Finally, *remember that many windfalls—a gambling win or a contest (but not most inheritances)—are subject to income tax.* All too many people have delighted in their great good luck until they had to pay the tax bill. How much of this money is really yours, and how much belongs to Uncle Sam? This can be particularly difficult if what you've won isn't a liquid asset. The $30,000 car you've won at a local contest can become a heavy millstone indeed when you realize that you owe federal, state, and possibly local taxes. (See *The Ernst & Young Tax Guide*, published annually by John Wiley & Sons, Inc., under "Prizes and Awards" for more details.)

3

BUILDING WEALTH THROUGH INVESTMENT PLANNING

- **Set Your Financial Goals**
- **Understand Investment Vehicles**

Investments play a significant role in your ability to accumulate and preserve wealth. However, it's crucial to realize from the start that *no single investment is right for everyone.* You have unique financial needs, goals, and personal circumstances that determine which specific investments are appropriate for your individual situation. To accumulate wealth effectively, selecting appropriate investment vehicles is a must. Thus the most important financial planning question isn't, "What's the best investment?" but rather, "How do I determine which investments are best for *me*?"

Here's a six-step process to assist you in answering that question.

- *Step 1*: Set your financial goals.
- *Step 2*: Understand investment vehicles.
- *Step 3*: Understand financial markets and concepts.
- *Step 4*: Develop an investment strategy.
- *Step 5*: Implement your strategy.
- *Step 6*: Monitor your investments.

In this chapter and the next two, we'll walk through all six steps of the investment process. In this chapter we address Steps 1 and 2; in Chapter 4 we explain Steps 3 and 4; and in Chapter 5 we discuss Steps 5 and 6.

STEP 1 | SET YOUR FINANCIAL GOALS

The first step of the investment planning process is to determine where you're coming from, financially speaking, before you commit yourself to specific investments. This determination is necessary before you decide what investment choices suit your purposes.

10 Big Mistakes in Investing — #3 Jumping on the bandwagon

The investment that all your friends are excited about may not be right for *you*.

Your financial goals will determine what investments you should make. The more specific your financial goals, the more easily you can select investments that will help you meet those goals. Imagine, for instance, that you state one of your financial goals as follows: "I want to be able to retire some day." A more specific goal would be: "I want to retire at age 55 and be able to spend $50,000 in today's dollars annually for the rest of my life." From a financial planning standpoint, these two statements are worlds apart. Merely setting the goal of eventual retirement doesn't indicate what you need to do to achieve your goal. The second statement, however, lets you begin to project how much money you'll need for retiring in the manner you desire. From there you can determine the level of annual savings and the mix of investments that can help you accumulate funds for retirement.

Here are four factors that determine how you should set your financial goals:

- Your investment time horizon
- Your priorities
- Quantification
- Your personal investment profile

Your Investment Time Horizon

The length of time that you have to reach your goal is considered by many advisors as the most important factor in determining which type of investment is best suited to meet that goal. Investments that are appropriate for funding a long-term goal (e.g., retirement in 15 years) would generally not be appropriate for a shorter-term goal (e.g., saving money to buy a vacation home in 3 years). The reverse is true as well. We talk more about time horizon when we discuss the types of investments later.

Your Priorities

You must also prioritize your financial goals and decide which are necessary and which are merely desirable. Depending on the time frame, you may need to invest for your highest-priority goals first, then wait until you feel confident you'll attain them before investing to meet lower-priority goals.

Quantification

After determining your financial priorities, you should develop financial projections and calculate different alternative scenarios to quantify your goals. From these calculations, you can then establish the amount you can save and what rate of return is necessary from your investments to assure that you'll achieve your goals.

Quantifying your goals involves projecting income and expenses, for both the short and long terms. Using these projections, you can establish parameters for funding multiple goals; lacking these parameters, however, you simply won't have enough information to allow for informed decision-making.

What are your options for quantifying goals? The most common means are:

- Seeking assistance from financial advisors
- Using financial planning software

The first of these options is the more traditional; the second has become increasingly common in recent years. Whichever method you use, however, you must know where you stand and where you want to go in specific terms.

Your Personal Investment Profile

Your investment profile is the key to determining which types of investments are right for you. Your investment profile is shaped by:

- Your age and the stage in your career
- Your need for liquidity
- The size of your portfolio
- Your cash flow needs
- Your income tax bracket
- Your required rate of return
- Your risk tolerance

Your Age and the Stage in Your Career. Your age and the stage in your career are important elements in determining which investments are right for you. Generally, if you are young and in the early stages of your career, you have time on your side. You may be able to experience a loss and recover through years of additional savings. Your peak earnings lie years ahead of you. If you are older, investment loss can be devastating. You may be retiring in a couple of years and have little time to replace your losses with additional savings.

Remember, however, that the time horizon to the goal is the critical factor regardless of your age. If the time horizon to the goal is 3 years, the appropriate investment can be the same for the 30-year-old investor as for the 60-year-old investor, based on their risk tolerance.

E
X
A
M
P
L
E

■ Marilyn, Joshua, and Ted represent three generations in a family with a long history of personal investing. Marilyn is 26 and just a few years into her business career. She enjoys the challenges of investing and feels confident that time is on her side, so she tolerates investment risks that Joshua, her 53-year-old father, once took as well but now avoids. While Marilyn invests 10% in cash, 20% in bonds, and 70% in stocks, Joshua feels more comfortable with 10% in cash, 40% in bonds, and 50% in stocks, which provide a lower expected return but have lower risk as well. As for Ted—74 now and reliant on his investments for a significant portion of his income—he restructured his portfolio to 10% cash, 60% bonds, and 30% stocks before retiring. This asset allocation helps provide stable cash flow. ■

Your Need for Liquidity. As noted earlier, a liquid asset is one that can be converted to cash in a short period of time without loss of principal. You can tell whether an investment is liquid or not depending on how certain and how fast you'll get all your money back. (For example, money market funds are highly liquid.) You may require higher investment liquidity to cover large near-term expenditures (such as tuition for a son or daughter about to enter college) or to fund your contingency fund.

The Size of Your Portfolio. By the size of your portfolio, we mean the total value of your investments. The size of your portfolio is both an absolute and a relative number. Most of us would agree that a $400,000 portfolio is large in absolute terms. However, if you are retired, have no pension benefit, and require $40,000 a year to live in your current lifestyle, your $400,000 portfolio is small relative to your living expense requirements.

Your portfolio's size will dictate the manner in which to invest. For example, if you have $50,000 to invest in stocks, buying the stocks of only a few individual companies may not be appropriate. You simply cannot achieve sufficient market diversification. Mutual funds that invest in stocks would be a better investment choice.

The size of your portfolio will also indicate the types of investments to include in your portfolio. A large portfolio may give you the ability to purchase certain investments that, because of their risk, minimum purchase requirement, or liquidity characteristics, are inappropriate for a smaller portfolio. Investing 20% of your investments in illiquid assets such as real estate may be all right if you have a large portfolio to invest but may not be appropriate if you have only $50,000.

But, again, remember that everything is relative. The retired person discussed above who requires $40,000 a year to live probably cannot afford illiquidity despite his $400,000 portfolio. That's why it is important to sketch out your entire personal investment profile before you invest.

Your Cash Flow Needs. If you need to supplement your cash flow, investments providing current income (such as dividends or interest payments) may be preferable to those whose return comes largely from capital appreciation. Significant excess cash flow decreases the need for liquidity; shortages increase the need.

Cash flow may not be your primary concern right now, but you should always keep it in mind. When you restructure your portfolio just before retirement, for example, cash flow may be your main consideration as you will no longer receive a check to meet your expenses. Another consideration: If you have real estate in your portfolio, cash flow will be more important to you than to someone whose portfolio contains only stocks and bonds, since there's always the possibility of negative cash flow when you own real estate. (See Chapter 6 for discussions of real estate and investing for retirement.)

Your Income Tax Bracket. Your income tax bracket determines how much of your taxable investment income you can keep. Being in a high tax bracket may lead you to invest in more tax-favored investments; being in a low tax bracket allows you to realize a greater after-tax return from investments that are fully taxable.

Keeping taxes in mind when making your investments can really pay off. Assume, for instance, that you have $10,000 to invest and have two alternatives that differ only in their taxation:

1. 6% tax-exempt interest income
2. 7% taxable interest income

If your tax bracket (federal, state, and local) is 30%, your $10,000 investment would grow to $32,071 in 20 years with alternative 1, compared to $26,032 with alternative 2 (net of tax). This calculation assumes that your investment earnings are reinvested each year. You'd be over $6,000 better off by taking advantage of the tax-favored investment.

The table below shows the yield you would have to earn on a taxable bond in order to generate the same after-tax earnings as a tax-exempt bond would provide at a correspondingly lower yield.

Equivalent Yield Needed from a Taxable Bond

Tax-Exempt Yield	Your Combined Federal, State & Local Marginal Tax Bracket						
	28%	31%	33%	36%	39.6%	42%	46%
4.00	5.56	5.80	5.97	6.25	6.62	6.90	7.41
4.50	6.25	6.52	6.72	7.03	7.45	7.76	8.33
5.00	6.94	7.25	7.46	7.81	8.28	8.62	9.26
5.50	7.64	7.97	8.21	8.59	9.11	9.48	10.19
6.00	8.33	8.70	8.96	9.38	9.93	10.34	11.11
6.50	9.03	9.42	9.70	10.16	10.76	11.21	12.04
7.00	9.72	10.14	10.45	10.94	11.59	12.07	12.96

Your Required Rate of Return. This is the amount of total return you need from your investments to meet your financial goals. For example, you may determine that to retire as planned, you need an average annual return of 8% per year, assuming that inflation is 5% per year or less. This required return will help you determine the types of investments you need to meet your financial goals.

Your Risk Tolerance. This factor relates to the degree that risk influences your choice of investments. If you're like most investors, you're risk-averse: You don't want to take any more risk than is absolutely necessary. However, the phrase "No risk, no reward" applies here just as in other situations. The degree of risk you'll accept will affect your potential return. If you have a low risk tolerance, you may tend to avoid investments you perceive as risky; however, you'll pay a price in the return you will achieve.

Identify Your Investment Objectives

As you develop your investment profile, you should also identify your specific investment objectives. (*Note*: Investment objectives differ from financial goals.) Investment objectives relate to the attributes you decide you need in your investments. The following checklist on investment objectives will help you decide which are most important to you, and in what priority.

Investment Objectives. What are your investment objectives? Rank the following objectives numerically to find out.

- Liquidity (*instant cash with no loss of principal*) _____
- Current income (*maximize income today*) _____
- Future income (*maximize income in future periods*) _____
- Inflation protection (*protection against loss of purchasing power*) _____
- Capital growth (*real increase in value of assets*) _____
- Safety of principal (*minimal risk of losing principal*) _____
- Diversification (*minimize risk by investing in a variety of assets*) _____

- Marketability (*convertible quickly to cash, but could have loss of principal*)   _____
- Ease of management (*relief from day-to-day decisions*)   _____

However, keep in mind that *no single investment can satisfy all these objectives*. While many investments can help you achieve one or more investment objectives, meeting all at once means investing in a variety of investment vehicles. Each investor's investment objectives are different. For this reason, you should select the mix of investments that's most appropriate for you.

STEP 2	## UNDERSTAND INVESTMENT VEHICLES

The next step is to review and understand the major investment vehicles:

- Cash
- Bonds
- Stocks

In later chapters we also review other investment types, such as gold, real estate, and foreign securities.

Category 1: Cash Investments

You may think you know what cash is—that crinkly green stuff in your wallet—but in fact, *cash* refers to investments with a high level of liquidity and little or no risk to principal.

> **Principal:** *the sum of money you invest.*

In general, cash investments are short-term interest-bearing securities and deposit accounts that offer liquidity, safety of principal, and current interest. The cash investments that individual investors use most frequently include savings accounts, certificates of deposit (CDs), money market funds, and Series EE bonds. In addition, many employees elect to invest some of their 401(k) plan investments in the guaranteed investment contracts (GIC) option. This is also a cash type of investment.

The FDIC generally insures passbook accounts, money market deposit accounts, and CDs issued by member banks and savings and loans. There is federal deposit insurance for credit unions that differs slightly from that provided by the FDIC. You should inquire about this protection when you open an account at a new institution to confirm your balances will be covered. Because the maximum protection of $100,000 is determined by how the account is titled on the institution's records, you should also consider the name (or names) placed on new accounts to avoid losing deposit insurance protection.

The following is a rundown of frequently used cash investments:

- Passbook accounts
- Money market deposit accounts
- U.S. Government Series EE bonds
- Certificates of Deposit (CDs)
- Money market mutual funds
- U.S. Treasury bills
- Guaranteed investment contracts (GICs)

Here are some of the kinds of cash investments you can obtain from specific sources:

Cash Investments Available Through Banks and Thrift Institutions

- Passbook accounts
- Money market deposit accounts

- Series EE bonds
- CDs

Cash Investments Available Through Brokerage Firms

- Brokered CDs
- Money market funds
- U.S. Treasury bills

Cash Investments Available Elsewhere

- Money market funds—from mutual fund companies
- Guaranteed investment contracts—through participation in many 401(k) plans

Now let's consider each of these cash investments.

Passbook Accounts. You can obtain passbook accounts through most banks, savings and loan institutions, and credit unions. Typically, they pay a relatively low rate of interest. Passbook accounts are liquid, but they generally do not include check-writing privileges.

Money Market Deposit Accounts. Generally paying a higher rate of interest than passbook accounts, money market deposit accounts typically require a minimum deposit, and they may charge fees if your balance falls below a minimum requirement. Money market deposit accounts, unlike money market mutual funds (discussed later), are federally insured. Because of their high degree of liquidity, however, money market deposit accounts generally return a yield somewhat lower than other less liquid, longer-term cash investments, such as certificates of deposit.

U.S. Government Series EE Bonds. Also referred to as savings bonds, these are cash investments that can provide relatively high interest rates and tax advantages. Series EE bonds:

- Are purchased at 50% of the face amount
- Range in face value from $50 to $10,000
- Are limited to $30,000 face value per year total purchase for any one person
- Increase in value, based on a floating interest rate equal to 85% of the average return on 5-year Treasury securities, if held for at least 5 years
- Cannot be redeemed any time before the first 6 months
- Do not require federal taxes to be paid on the accrued income until the bonds are redeemed, unless the owner elects otherwise
- May result in no tax on the interest income if the bond proceeds are used to pay qualified education expenses, provided that the taxpayer's adjusted gross income doesn't exceed certain levels

The interest on Series EE bonds—which is already exempt from state and local income taxes—may be exempt from federal income tax as well if you pay tuition at colleges, universities, and qualified technical schools during the year you redeem the bonds. The exemption applies not only to your children's education but also to your own higher education.

This educational benefit is straightforward, but there are restrictions. To qualify, the bonds:

- Must have been issued after December 31, 1989, to persons who are at least 24 years old
- Must be issued in either one or both parents' names (who are at least 24 years old) if the bonds are to benefit dependent children

> - Must be redeemed in a year that the bond owner pays qualified educational expenses, which are tuition and fees, to an eligible educational institution
>
> In addition, the bonds will be fully exempt from federal income tax only if your income is below certain limits, *and* the exemption applies only to the extent of the qualified amount of tuition and fees you've paid during the year.
>
> For more information on Series EE bonds, contact: Office of Public Affairs, U.S. Savings Bonds Division, Washington, DC 20226 (www.publicdebt.treas.gov).

Certificates of Deposit (CDs). CDs are deposits made with a bank or savings and loan for a specified period of time, usually a minimum of 3 or 6 months. The institution generally pays a fixed rate of interest for the term of the certificate, with rates generally increasing with the amount and term of the deposit. You may also be able to purchase CDs with variable interest rates. Early withdrawal may result in a significant penalty.

Because they aren't as liquid as money market deposit accounts, new CDs should pay interest at a rate higher than money market accounts at the same institution. Shop around for the best rates—banks and other institutions aren't uniform in the rates they offer. Also, don't limit your search to these institutions alone. Most stock brokerage houses sell CDs issued by banks and savings and loans. Such CDs are also federally insured. Brokered CDs provide several additional advantages:

- A *secondary market*, which allows you to sell your CD before maturity without incurring any early withdrawal penalty.
- *Potentially higher interest rates* than are available at your local bank.

- *Geographic diversification.* Brokerage houses offer CDs issued by banks and thrifts located throughout the country; this provides you with another sort of diversification.

Money Market Mutual Funds. One of the most popular cash investments, money market mutual funds are funds that invest in U.S. Treasury bills, commercial paper, jumbo CDs, and other short-term interest-bearing securities. Securities held by money market funds normally have an average term to maturity of approximately 30 to 90 days. The interest earned on money market mutual funds is often higher than that earned on passbook savings accounts and money market deposit accounts.

Money market mutual funds don't have federal insurance protection; however, they lack the risk of uninsured bank accounts. One advantage of money market mutual funds is that you may be able to increase your after-tax rate of return for the cash portion of your portfolio by investing in tax-exempt money market mutual funds that invest only in short-term municipal securities. Both tax-exempt and taxable money market funds frequently offer services such as check-writing privileges and/or the ability to telephone-transfer funds from your money market mutual fund to another mutual fund in the same family of funds. Consider these conveniences when selecting your money market fund, as they can be more important than a slightly greater rate of return.

U.S. Treasury Bills. Investors who have large cash balances and who are interested in maximum safety and interest income that is free of state and local taxes should consider U.S. Treasury bills. U.S. Treasury bills are sold on a discount basis. The difference between the discount price and the maturity value is considered the interest income. U.S. Treasury bills are purchased through weekly Federal Reserve Board auctions in minimum denominations of $10,000. They have 3-, 6-, or 12-month stated maturities. U.S. Treasury bills are also traded on the secondary market. Interest on U.S. Treasury bills is taxable for federal income tax purposes at the time of sale or maturity, but interest is not taxed at the state level.

Guaranteed Investment Contracts (GICs). GICs are fixed-interest-bearing contracts typically issued by insurance companies and purchased by 401(k) plans. The interest rates paid on GICs often dramatically exceed those paid on other cash investments. They tend to have 3- to 5-year maturities, but the value of a GIC fund doesn't fluctuate with changes in interest rates. GICs are backed by the issuing company. That's not as safe as federal insurance protection; however, barring default, your principal will remain safe even when interest rates increase.

Comparison of Cash Investments

Investment	Possible check writing	Interest	Possible tax advantages	Liquidity
Passbook accounts	No	Low	No	High
Money market deposit accounts	Yes	Low	No	High
Series EE bonds	No	High	Yes	Low
Certificates of deposit	No	Medium	No	Low
Money market mutual funds	Yes	Medium	Yes	High
U.S. Treasury bills	No	Medium	Yes	Medium
Guaranteed investment contracts	No	High	NA	NA

Category 2: Bonds

Bonds are debt instruments, typically issued by a government or a corporation. When you purchase a bond, you (the investor) are granting a loan to the issuer. You put up current cash in exchange for regular interest payments (except in the case of zero-coupon bonds) and the return of the principal at maturity. A *zero-coupon bond* doesn't have regular interest payments; instead, it's purchased at a discount and matures at a higher face value, similar to a U.S. Series EE Bond.

Given these characteristics, bonds are typically appropriate in two situations:

- If you are seeking steady cash flow
- If you don't have an immediate need for the principal invested

Moreover, bonds can be used to diversify your portfolio and can be excellent vehicles for funding short- to intermediate-term goals, since you can match the bond's maturity to the date you need funds for the goal. An example: Your retirement is 5 years away. You want to purchase a second home at that time. Under these circumstances, a 5-year bond ensures that the principal amount will be available when you retire (assuming that the issuing institution does not default).

Generally speaking, the longer the maturity of a bond, the higher the interest rate. That's because enticing you to commit money for a longer period requires the issuers to pay a comparatively higher rate. Before selecting a bond, you should therefore consider whether the issuer is offering sufficient additional interest for the length of time you're investing your money.

Who has issued the bond is also important, since this will determine the extent to which the interest paid by the bond is taxable. For example, interest paid by state or local governments (i.e., for municipal bonds) is exempt from federal taxes. Another factor: Different issuers may have higher or lower credit ratings, which means that the possibility of default varies from one issuer to the next.

Two organizations—Moody's and Standard & Poor's—rate the ability of issuers to repay principal and make interest payments, using bond ratings shown in the table below. These organizations employ financial analysts to review the issuers' creditworthiness at the time of the investment's initial sale as well as at periodic intervals. The rating assigned is an independent indication of the offering's investment quality: You should review it before you invest in bonds.

In addition to default risk, bonds are subject to possible loss of value if interest rates rise. As interest rates rise, the value of bonds falls: Conversely, if interest rates fall, the value of bonds

BOND RATINGS

Moody's	Standard & Poor's	Meaning of Rating
Aaa	AAA	Best quality
Aa	AA	High quality
A	A	Upper-medium quality
Baa	BBB	Medium quality
Ba	BB	Below investment grade
B	B	Low grade
Caa	CCC	Very risky
Ca	CC	Highly speculative
C	C	Lowest grade
D	D	In default

rises. The closer the bond is to maturity, the less price fluctuation you can expect because (barring default) you will receive full face value at the date of maturity. Consequently the longer the bond's term to maturity, the greater the risk to its interest rate and the greater the risk of default.

> **Maturity:** *the date on which a loan or bond comes due and is to be paid off.*
> **Default risk:** *the possibility that a company or other bond issuer will fail to make payment on its debts.*
> **Interest rate risk:** *the risk that interest rates will rise, thus lowering the market value of bonds issued earlier.*

The bonds we'll consider are:

- Corporate bonds
- U.S. government securities
- Municipal bonds
- Mortgage-backed securities

Corporate Bonds. Corporate bonds can be issued in many different forms. They can be secured by assets, or they can be an unsecured promise to repay an amount borrowed. Debentures are unsecured promissory notes supported by the corporation's general creditworthiness. In the case of default or bankruptcy, this unsecured debt is redeemed only after the secured creditors' claims are satisfied. Debentures that are *subordinated* have more risk of default because they are paid off after regular unsecured debt.

 What are junk bonds?

 Junk bonds are corporate bonds characterized by low quality ratings and consequently higher-than-average interest rates.

Typically, corporate bonds pay their holders interest semi-annually. The interest earned on the bonds is subject to federal tax and to the investor's resident state and local income tax, if any. These bonds nearly always pay higher interest rates than government bonds, since there is a higher risk of default. The interest rates offered vary widely depending on the issuing corporation's financial strength. The weaker the company, the greater the risk and the higher the interest rate.

 What's the best way to reduce the risk of the bonds I buy?

 Purchase high-quality bonds—A- to triple A–rated bonds— and make sure that they mature in no more than 5 years. Then your bonds are less likely to be subject to interest rate risk or default risk.

The term to maturity of the bond will also influence its interest rate. The longer the term, the greater the risk of default and interest rate risk. Consequently, longer-term bonds typically pay higher interest than do shorter-term bonds. This general rule does not apply in times where interest rates are expected to decline. The following table shows the effect of a one percentage point change in interest rates on the value of bonds with varying maturities and interest rates.

WHAT IF INTEREST RATES CHANGE BY 1%?

Current interest rate	Maturity: Bond's Percentage Price Change					
	3 months	1 yr	5 yr	10 yr	20 yr	30 yr
12%	0.25	1.0	3.7	5.7	7.5	8.1
11%	0.25	1.0	3.8	6.0	8.0	8.7
10%	0.25	1.0	3.9	6.2	8.6	9.5
9%	0.25	1.0	4.0	6.5	9.2	10.3
8%	0.25	1.0	4.1	6.8	9.9	11.3

Note: *The table estimates the percentage price change of a bond paying interest semiannually. It assumes that the bond's coupon is roughly the same as the current interest rate and that the bond is priced to maturity rather than to a call date.*

Keep in mind, too, that many corporate bonds have a call feature that enables the corporation to redeem them prior to maturity. You should consider this feature when selecting bonds to meet your desired average term to maturity. This call feature may cause the bond to be redeemed at an amount other than its par value on a date other than its date of maturity.

U.S. Government Securities. Federal government securities are similar to corporate securities in many respects. However, some important differences exist as well. U.S. government securities are generally considered the safest form of investing (from a standpoint of risk of nonpayment of principal or interest) because of the government's taxing authority. This safety means that the yields are lower than those of comparable-term corporate securities.

U.S. Treasury notes and Treasury bonds are government debts distinguished primarily by their terms to maturity. U.S. Treasury notes are intermediate-term obligations that mature in 2 to 10 years. You can purchase 2- and 3-year notes for a minimum of $5,000, while longer-term notes have a $1,000 minimum investment requirement. Treasury bonds are long-term debt maturing in 10 to 30 years. The minimum available investment in long-term Treasury bonds is $1,000. Interest on U.S. Treasury notes and bonds is paid semiannually and is subject to federal income taxation, but exempt from state and local tax.

Among the most popular forms of government securities are *zero-coupon Treasury securities* and *agency bonds*.

Zero-Coupon Treasury Securities. Zero-coupon Treasury securities are sold by the U.S. Treasury Department under its STRIPs program and by major brokerage houses under such names as CATs, LIONs, and TIGRs. The semiannual interest coupons are "stripped off." Consequently, these bonds do not pay interest currently; however, a lump-sum amount is paid at maturity equal to the bond's face value. These bonds are sold at a deep discount to face value. For example, you might pay only $5,000 for a bond that will pay you $10,000 in 10 years. The discounted purchase price makes up for the fact that the bond pays no current interest. However, since interest income is taxed as it accrues over the term of the bond, "zeros" produce taxable income without current cash payments of interest.

A new type of Treasury zero-coupon bond, known as the "I-Bond" is available as of September 1, 1998. I-Bonds are sold at face value and grow with inflation-indexed earnings for up to 30 years. You can invest from $50 to $30,000 a year. But, like Series EE bonds, the interest is not taxable until you cash them in.

Agency Bonds. Similar to U.S. Treasury obligations, agency bonds are issued by government agencies other than the Treasury itself. They resemble Treasury bonds in having maturities ranging from short-term to long-term, paying interest subject to federal taxation semiannually, and having an active secondary market. Agency bonds often provide investors with slightly higher interest income than that of comparable U.S. Treasuries. For example, a 5-year note issued by the Federal Farm Credit Bank may pay 5.55% in interest, at the same time a 5-year U.S. Treasury note pays 5.4%. While the Federal Farm Credit Bank debt is not backed by the full faith and credit of the U.S. government (as U.S. Treasury obligations are), the federal government is unlikely to permit the Federal Farm Credit Bank to default on its debt in 5 years.

Municipal Bonds. State and local governments issue municipal bonds, usually to finance long-term projects. Municipal notes such as "tax anticipation" notes are for short-term needs. Similar to federal securities, municipal bonds are usually not secured by a tangible asset; rather, they are debts payable from the state or local government's general tax revenue. These bonds are known as "general obligation" bonds. In some instances, revenue from a specific source may be used for servicing the indebtedness. Such bonds are appropriately named "revenue" bonds.

10 Big Mistakes in Investing — #4 Misunderstanding the meaning of "high yield"

This doesn't mean more interest income without any additional risk. Usually, it applies to a junk bond or a mutual fund investing in lower quality bonds.

Municipal obligations differ from federal government issues in that they are subject to the risk of default. Like corporate debt securities, municipal obligations are rated according to their creditworthiness. A triple-A rating indicates the lowest risk of default. The lower the risk of default, the lower the required interest rate.

Next we look at some other features of municipal bonds that influence their levels of risk and return.

Insurance Features. Some issues of municipal bonds are insured against failure to repay principal by an independent insurance company. Bonds with this insurance feature usually pay lower interest than do similar uninsured bonds because the insurance reduces their risk of default.

Pre-refunding. Municipal bonds that are "pre-refunded" are also considered to be subject to low default risk. The reason is that the municipality issuing your municipal bond has purchased U.S. government securities with the same term to maturity as your bond. Held in a special account, these U.S. government bonds essentially provide collateral for the bond you hold, thus providing security against default.

Call Features. Many municipal bonds have call features enabling the municipality to redeem them prior to maturity. This may result in prepayment risk, since the issuer may return your principal to you when interest rates are lower.

Interest Rate Risk. All municipal obligations are subject to interest rate risk similar to that of other bonds. The longer the term to maturity, the higher the interest rate risk and consequently the higher the interest rate.

Municipal bonds and mutual funds that invest in municipal bonds traditionally have been an important part of the high-bracket taxpayers' investment portfolio. One of the main reasons is their tax-favored status. Here are some of the relevant issues:

Federal Income Tax Status. The semiannual interest payments of bonds issued by state and local governments are generally free from federal income tax. This provides a potentially greater after-tax rate of return than for comparable taxable investments.

Alternative Minimum Tax. The interest on some state and local "private activity" bonds is subject to the alternative minimum tax (AMT). Bonds issued for normal governmental purposes (running the government) remain tax-exempt for regular tax as well as for AMT purposes. If you aren't subject to the AMT, consider buying private activity municipal bonds that aren't AMT exempt, because they typically have a higher interest rate. (See both the *Ernst & Young Tax Guide* and *Tax Saver's Guide*, published annually by John Wiley & Sons, Inc., for more information on the AMT).

Resident State Income Tax. The interest earned on municipal bonds and funds is frequently subject to the investor's resident state income tax. However, most states don't levy a tax on the interest income paid on their own governmental entities' issues.

Mortgage-Backed Securities.
Mortgage-backed securities are debt issues secured by pools of home mortgages. Mortgage loans made by banks and savings and loan associations are "pooled" together; units in the pool are then sold to investors, who receive distributions (payments of interest and principal) as the loans are paid off. Mortgage-backed securities can be issued by federal as well as private institutions. "Pass-through" is the generic name given to any pool of mortgages that provides periodic payments of interest and principal to investors. It generally refers to mortgage pools established by the following agencies.

- *GNMA:* the Government National Mortgage Association ("Ginnie Mae")
- *FHLMC:* the Federal Home Loan Mortgage Corporation ("Freddie Mac")
- *FNMA:* the Federal National Mortgage Association ("Fannie Mae")

Two other mortgage-backed securities are *collateralized mortgage obligations* (CMOs) and *real estate mortgage investment conduits* (REMICs). Before investing in these securities, or mutual funds that invest in mortgage-backed securities, it is important to understand their risks as well as return potential. CMOs separate the mortgages held in the pool into different groups (called tranches) based on maturity dates. The tranche selected by the investor dictates whether the principal payments will be accelerated or postponed. (Sophisticated investment knowledge is required to understand the risk and return characteristics of the various tranches.)

Mortgage-backed securities are not without risk. Although the risk of default is minimal, the risk of prepayment (particularly in periods of falling mortgage rates) can be substantial. This causes larger amounts of principal to be returned to you when interest rates drop and lowers the expected return.

Category 3: Stocks

Stocks represent an ownership interest in a company. As an owner, you'll realize a positive return from the investment only to the extent that the company's earnings are more than sufficient to satisfy the claims of the company's creditors.

After a company has paid all of its bills each year (including any payments to bondholders), the remaining cash flow belongs to the shareholders. For this reason, a stock investment is considered a residual interest in the company. This residual interest may be paid to shareholders each year in the form of dividends, or it may be reinvested in the continuing operations of the company, thereby increasing the value of the stockholder's shares over time (resulting in growth and capital gains). Dividends generally are fully taxable when you, the shareholder, receive them: Capital gains are generally not taxed until the stock is sold. At that time, the gain may be taxed at favorable rates, depending on the tax law in effect at the time. The most common form of stock is *common stock*. However, preferred stocks offer investors another option that is typically less risky than common stocks.

Common Stocks. Common stocks can help accumulate wealth in two ways:

- They can provide income through dividends, which are distributions to shareholders of corporate earnings.
- They can appreciate in value, generally as a result of successful company operations or the prospect of successful future operations.

Keep in mind that the possibility of capital appreciation is mirrored by the possibility of a decline in the value of your investment. Risk varies from stock to stock and from industry to industry. See Chapter 4 for a discussion of these factors.

Where can I find information about stocks?

 Here are some good sources, in both print and electronic media:

In Print

Financial newspapers. *The Wall Street Journal, Barron's,* and *Investor's Business Daily*, in addition to the **stock listings in most daily newspapers**.

Company annual reports. Information about a company, usually including audited financial data.

Analysts' reports. Information about specific companies, often with recommendations to buy, hold, or sell specific stocks.

Moody's Investors Services. Specific publications include *Moody's Manuals* (compendiums of current and historical data on several thousand companies), *The Handbook of Common Stocks* (data on roughly 1,000 stocks), and *Annual Dividend Report* (a record of publicly traded companies' current dividend payments). Available from brokers or directly from Moody's, 99 Church Street, New York, NY 10007-2701. Phone: (800) 342-5647.

Standard & Poor's Corporation. Various publications, including S&P *Stock Reports* (current and historical analytical data pertaining to domestic stocks) and *Stock Guide* (a compendium of data on more than 5,000 stocks). Available from libraries, brokers, or directly from S&P, 65 Broadway, 8th floor, New York, NY 10006. Phone: (800) 221-5277.

Value Line Investment Survey. Information on approximately 1,700 stocks and closed-end funds, plus analysis and recommendations. Available from libraries or directly from Value Line Publishing, 220 E. 42nd St, New York, NY 10011. Phone: (800) 633-2252.

On-Line Investment Information

America Online, Inc. Stock and mutual fund quotes and other current investment data. Produced by America Online, Inc. (www.aol.com).

CompuServe. Stock and mutual fund quotes and historical data. Produced by CompuServe, Inc. (www.compuserve.com).

Dow Jones Market Monitor. Market quotes, investment news, data bases, investment information security snapshots, and abstracts of analysts' research reports. Produced by Dow Jones & Co., Inc. (www.dowjones.com).

Microsoft Network. Stock quotes and investment news and information. Produced by Microsoft (www.msn.com).

Prodigy. Stock quotes and investment news and information. Produced by Prodigy Internet (www.prodigy.com).

Reuters Money Network. CD, stock, mutual fund quotes, and investment news and information. Produced by Reuters Limited (www.reuters.com).

Value Screen III. Current data on market prices. Produced by Value Line Publishing (www.valueline.com).

Publicly traded stocks (i.e., stocks listed on the NYSE, AMEX, and NASDAQ) are considered readily marketable investments because they can be converted into cash quickly. Since they are subject to potential loss of principal, however, they aren't considered liquid. Nonpublicly traded stocks are generally regarded as nonmarketable because they are difficult to sell and the selling price is uncertain.

> **NYSE** (the New York Stock Exchange—known as "the Big Board"): the largest securities exchange in the United States.
> **AMEX** (the American Stock Exchange): the second-largest exchange, also located in New York City.
> **NASDAQ** (the National Association of Securities Dealers Automated Quotations): an automated information network that provides brokers and dealers with price quotations on OTC (over-the-counter) stocks.

Publicly traded common stock can be segregated into several broad categories based upon the type of return offered (i.e., dividends vs. capital appreciation), financial stability of the company, industry of the company, and susceptibility to changes in stock value resulting from changes in market and economic conditions. In some cases, a stock will fit into more than one category. The following categories are one way to segregate stocks:

- Income stocks
- Growth stocks
- Cyclical stocks
- Defensive stocks
- Blue chip stocks

Market capitalization: *the per share price of a company multiplied by the number of shares outstanding.*
Large capitalization stocks: *the stock of companies with market capitalizations of more than $5 billion.*
Midcapitalization stocks: *the stock of companies with market capitalizations between $500 million and $5 billion.*
Small capitalization stocks: *the stock of companies with market capitalizations of less than $500 million.*

Let's consider briefly the characteristics of each category.

Income Stocks. Income stocks are those with a long and sustained record of paying high dividends. Generally, a company whose common stock falls into this category is in a fairly stable and mature industry (e.g., an electric utility company). These companies normally pay out a relatively high percentage of corporate earnings as dividends to common stockholders. Because these companies distribute (rather than reinvest) their earnings, their stocks are less likely to experience substantial capital appreciation: They are also more likely to be sensitive to interest rate fluctuations. Income stocks are particularly popular with people who need current cash flow from their stock investments.

Growth Stocks. Growth stocks are stocks that are expected to experience high rates of growth in operations and/or earnings.

These growth rates are usually substantially higher than the market averages. To support their high growth rates, these companies generally reinvest their earnings instead of distributing them as dividends. Growth stocks are generally much riskier than income stocks. The price of growth stocks tends to rise faster than that of other stocks, and their total return tends to be greater than that of income stocks. On the other hand, growth stocks are also more likely to suffer a price decline in a bear market. Stocks of companies in new and rapidly expanding industries—computers, engineering, and other high-technology industries—are frequently considered growth stocks.

Growth stocks don't fit especially well with an investment strategy calling for high current cash flow from investments and a high degree of investment principal stability. If your objectives include holding investments for long-term capital appreciation, and if you're willing to assume the risk of a stock performing poorly, investing a portion of your available funds in growth stocks may be appropriate.

Cyclical Stocks. Typically, cyclical stocks are stocks of companies whose earnings tend to follow the business cycle. Highly cyclical industries include oil and other natural resources, steel, and housing. Cyclical stocks are often more risky than stocks in companies less subject to changes in the business cycle. If you choose to invest in cyclical stocks, your objective is to purchase these stocks when you envision an economic upturn and sell them before an economic downturn.

Defensive Stocks. Defensive stocks are stocks that are, in a sense, countercyclical. Prices of these stocks tend to remain stable or perhaps rise during periods of economic downturn, while showing poorer results (in comparison to other stocks) during periods of economic upturn. Investors frequently use defensive stocks to balance their investment portfolio. Defensive stocks are well-established companies producing goods that are generally still in demand during an economic downturn, such as food, beverages, and pharmaceuticals.

10 Big Mistakes in Investing — #5
Refusing to let go

Some securities will never "come back." Even if they do, the rate of return you receive in the meantime may not rival what you would have gotten on an alternative investment.

Blue Chip Stocks. The stocks of the companies with the highest overall quality are those considered to be "blue chips." The companies with blue chip common stocks are financially stable companies with steady dividend-paying records during both good and bad years. They are usually the leaders within their industry or industry segment. Blue chip stocks include all of the Dow Jones 30 industrial companies, some utilities, and the stocks of other large and successful companies. Because of the blue chips' high level of quality and relative stability, many investors find them attractive long-term investments.

Preferred Stocks. Like the various kinds of common stock, preferred stocks also represent an ownership interest in a corporation. The reason preferred stocks are "preferred" is that the ownership of this type of stock allows the investor a right or preference not found in common stocks. Preferred stocks are in many ways a cross between common stocks and bonds. Preferred stocks represent an equity interest in a company, similar to common stocks, but they generally pay a fixed dividend, much as bonds pay interest. Prices of preferred stocks are particularly affected by interest rate changes.

The standard preferences inherent in preferred stocks include:

- *Dividend*: the right to be paid dividends before the common stockholders
- *Liquidation*: the right to receive the par value of the preferred stock on liquidation of the company prior to any distributions to common stockholders

Other features may include:

- *Voting*: the right to have more votes than those held by common stockholders or to elect more directors
- *Convertibility*: the right to exchange preferred shares for a fixed number of common shares
- *Cumulation of dividends*: if preferred dividends are ever omitted, all prior and current preferred dividends must be paid before common shareholders can be paid dividends
- *Participation*: the right to receive more than the stated amount of dividends under certain circumstances

In addition, preferred stocks may be subject to a "call" feature. This allows a corporation to "call in" or redeem the preferred shares at a fixed price.

Preferred stock almost always has a dividend yield in excess of the company's common stock. The higher current yield is required because most preferred stocks, unlike common stocks, do not participate in the earnings growth of companies. Thus the price of preferred stocks tends to be more stable than the price of common stocks. However, since preferred stocks are generally considered less risky than common stocks, they have commensurately lower total return expectations (dividends plus capital appreciation) and do not serve as an inflation hedge as do common stocks, except in the case of convertibles. Convertible preferred stock can serve as an inflation hedge because the value of the preferred stock will increase once the value of the underlying common stock exceeds a certain level.

4

BUILDING WEALTH THROUGH INVESTMENT PLANNING

- ■ **Understand Financial Markets and Concepts**
- ■ **Develop an Investment Strategy**

In addition to investment vehicles, several other concepts are important to your overview of the investment planning process. Understanding these concepts is Step 3 of the investment planning process; developing a strategy is Step 4.

STEP 3 — UNDERSTAND FINANCIAL MARKETS AND CONCEPTS

Before you match your investment profile and objectives to assets whose attributes suit your purposes, you'll need to understand certain financial concepts. The most important concepts for our purposes are:

- • Concept 1: Investment return
- • Concept 2: Investment risk
- • Concept 3: Portfolio structure

Concept 1: Investment Return

The return on investments comes in the form of income, capital appreciation, or both. The *total return* on an investment refers to the sum of these components. For example, let's suppose that you purchase a common stock for $100. After one year it produces $5 of dividends. The income return on the investment is $5/$100, or 5%—the current *yield*. If at the end of the year, the stock is also now worth $107, it has appreciated by 7% ($7/$100); this is its *growth rate*. The sum of these figures—in this example, 12%—is the stock's *total return*.

Depending on the type of investment you own, however, some or all of this return may be subject to federal and/or state income taxes. The amount you keep after paying taxes is called the *after-tax return*. The tax rate is the combined federal and state tax percentage (stated as a decimal) that you pay on the return component on which you are focusing (i.e., interest, dividends, and capital gains). (*Note*: Your tax on long-term capital gains may be lower due to the 20% maximum federal tax rate applicable to such income. Also, the tax on the growth part of return is deferred until the growth is recognized by selling the stock.)

Generating capital gains could be one of your big opportunities to save on taxes. Since the Taxpayer Relief Act of 1997, the tax benefit of long-term capital gains has again become substantial. Under this law, the top tax rate applicable to long-term capital gains is 20%, while the rate for ordinary income can go as high as 39.6%. If you can generate net capital gains instead of ordinary income, you can save up to 19.6% on your taxes. Also, with capital assets, you usually have some flexibility in controlling when you recognize the income or loss, because in most cases you determine when to sell the asset.

If you incur losses from the sale of a capital asset, you can deduct those losses to the extent they equal capital gains from the sale of other assets. If your losses exceed your gains, you can only deduct $3,000 ($1,500 if you are married and filing separately) of capital losses in a tax year against other income on Form 1040. You can carry losses forward and continue to deduct $3,000 ($1,500 if filing separately) annually against other income until your losses are used up or you die.

After-tax return is an effective way of comparing two investments that are taxed differently. Here's a quick way to calculate after-tax return:

$$\text{after-tax return} = \text{taxable return} \times (1 - \text{tax rate}) + \text{nontaxable income}$$

Let's say that you're comparing a U.S. Treasury bond paying 7% to a municipal bond paying 5%. To make a realistic comparison, you need to look beyond the coupon rate to see which bond offers you the highest after-tax return. The U.S. Treasury bond's interest is taxable at the federal level but not at the state level, whereas the municipal bond is tax-free at the federal level but could be taxable at the state level. Which investment provides the higher return depends on your individual income tax bracket and the tax laws of your state.

E
X
A
M
P
L
E

■ Tom is considering two different options for his $10,000 contingency fund. The first option—a taxable money market fund—currently pays 5% interest. The second option—a tax-exempt money market fund—currently pays 4% interest. If Tom's federal income tax rate is 28% and if he lives in a state that does not impose tax on investment income, Tom should compare his two investment options as follows:

taxable money market fund return after-tax
  income = 5% × (1−28%) = 3.6%
tax-exempt money market fund return after-tax
  income = 4%

The after-tax return for the tax-exempt fund is higher, therefore a better choice for Tom. ■

For a comparison of equivalent yields needed from a taxable bond, see page 69.

When calculating after-tax return, you should compare only bonds that are similar to each other in maturity and risk. You wouldn't compare a U.S. Treasury bond to a tax-exempt money market fund, for instance, because their maturities are different. Similarly, you can't compare an A-rated municipal bond to a U.S. Treasury bond; their default risks differ too substantially to allow the comparison.

Expected Return for the Future. Although it is relatively simple to calculate an investment's return over the *past* year, it's entirely different to try determining what an investment will return over the *next* year—or over the next 5 years or more. For most investments, the return in the previous year will be of little or no help in predicting the next year's return. Nevertheless, while past performance is no guarantee of future performance, longer-term historical data may at least provide an estimate (within an acceptable range) of an investment's (or portfolio's) future expected return.

10 Big Mistakes in Investing — #6
Focusing only on return

Here, as in so many other ways, there's no such thing as a free lunch.

Investment professionals sometimes estimate future return by using the average return an asset has produced over a 10-year, 20-year, or longer period. To determine an asset's average return we simply add the annual returns for each of the years we are reviewing and divide the result by the number of years. Based on history this return is what we expect to receive on average if we were to invest in that asset. The table below shows the historical average returns for various asset types from 1926, 1978, and 1988 (the longest period over which data are available) until the end of 1997. As a comparison we have included the average inflation rate over these periods as well. Subtracting the inflation rate produces the *real return* (which we discuss in a moment). We have used certain market indices as proxies for the historical performance of the asset type. For example, we have used the S&P 500 Index as a proxy for the historical performance of large capitalization domestic stocks.

HISTORICAL AVERAGE RETURNS			
	1926–1997	**1978–1997**	**1988–1997**
Treasury Bills	3.76%	7.29%	5.44%
Long-Term Government Bonds	5.22%	10.39%	11.32%
S&P 500	11.00%	16.65%	18.05%
Small Stocks	12.71%	17.71%	16.46%
International Stocks	NA	14.38%	6.56%
Inflation	3.10%	4.89%	3.41%

You can see that an investment in Treasury bills produced an average annual return of 3.77% since 1926. Since the average rate of return is just that—*an average*—you wouldn't necessarily receive a return of 3.77% every year from Treasury bills. In some years you would receive a higher return, and in other years you would receive a lower return. The next table shows how much you would have accumulated (before taxes) at the end of 1997 if you had invested $1 (with earnings reinvested) in each asset type in 1926, in 1978, or in 1988.

Because one of the primary goals of investing is to maintain the purchasing power of your capital, it's useful when estimating future returns to consider only the return in excess of inflation. This return is called the *real rate of return*. The third table shows the real rates of return for various asset classes over the same time periods as the two earlier tables.

VALUE OF $1 INVESTED IN VARIOUS ASSETS			
	1926–1997	1978–1997	1988–1997
Treasury Bills	$14.25	$4.08	$1.70
Long-Term Government Bonds	$39.07	$7.22	$2.92
S&P 500	$1,828.33	$21.75	$5.25
Small Stocks	$5,519.97	$26.10	$4.59
International Stocks	NA	$14.70	$1.89

REAL RATES OF RETURN			
	1926–1997	1978–1997	1988–1997
Treasury Bills	0.64%	2.29%	1.96%
Long-Term Government Bonds	2.06%	5.25%	7.65%
S&P 500	7.66%	11.21%	14.16%
Small Stocks	9.32%	12.23%	12.62%
International Stocks	NA	9.03%	3.01%

Concept 2: Investment Risk

Although return is an important aspect of determining whether an investment is appropriate, it's equally important to consider the risk associated with an investment. Each type of investment offers a different level or type of return; similarly, each investment has different associated risks.

When we say that an investment is risky, we generally mean that it may not return the average return that we expect each and every year. Although it may return more than we expect in some years, we are more concerned that it may return less than we expect in other years—and may even have a negative return (i.e., a loss of principal). A riskless security provides a rate of return that is predictable and has no chance of principal loss. Even if the total return were guaranteed, however, changing inflation rates would cause the real rate of return to vary, thus creating risk. Therefore a truly risk-less investment, in addition to having a guaranteed rate of return, would need to exist in a state of unchanging financial conditions. Based on this definition, *there can be no truly riskless investment*.

Although we can't eliminate risk altogether, we *can* minimize risk by using an appropriate investment strategy. And minimizing risk means understanding it and knowing how to measure it.

Quantifying Risk. Generally, we measure risk by the *volatility* of total return. The most risky assets are the most volatile—those whose annual returns fluctuate the most from what we expect to receive on average. These fluctuations are measured statistically using *standard deviation of return*. Standard deviation describes how far from the expected return (in either direction) we must go to cap-ture most of the *possible* returns that an investment might produce. One standard deviation in either direction of the average captures about two-thirds of all possible returns, with the remaining third split equally outside this range. Two standard deviations in either direction of the average captures about 95% of all possible returns.

> **Volatility:** *a state of being characterized by rapid change, in this case change of returns.*

The longer you hold any asset, the smaller its standard deviation. The implication is that returns become more predictable over longer periods of time. Thus, while the range of returns from the S&P 500 in any one year might be from 27.9% to 33% (one standard devia-tion), the range over 20 years is significantly smaller—from 6.34% to 15.26% (based on historical returns). This occurs because the greater-than-expected returns in "good" years counteract the worse-than-expected returns in "bad" years. An asset whose risk is unac-ceptable based on its one-year risk level may have acceptable risk if held 20 years. Therefore, your *investment horizon*—the length of time your funds will be invested—should play an important role in your choice of investments.

Types of Risk. Understanding investment risk allows you to select appropriate investments based on the amount and type of risk you're willing to tolerate. The degree of investment risk you'll accept is your *risk tolerance level*. Every investment is subject to some degree of risk. However, your risk tolerance level is an important aspect of identifying investments consistent with achieving your financial goals. The risk pyramid (shown below) is one way of illustrating the concept of risk.

Different kinds of investments are subject to different kinds of risk. The three major investment classes are cash, bonds, and stocks. The risks that typically affect each of them are:

Cash. The chief risk is *purchasing power risk*—the risk that the return on the investment or value of investment principal, as measured by purchasing power, will decrease due to inflation. Here's an example: If you invest in a cash investment that pays you 4% while the inflation rate is 3.75%, you'll actually lose purchasing power if your 4% income is subject to tax.

Bonds. Here you're betting on two outcomes:

- The interest rate will beat inflation.
- The interest will be paid *and* you'll get your money back.

Consequently, the relevant risks here are *interest rate risk* (i.e., will interest rates rise, thereby reducing your bonds' value?) and *default risk* (will the bonds' issuer *pay you back?*).

E
X
A
M
P
L
E

■ What happens if you take on a lot of risk and win or lose? Here are some typical outcomes:

Action	Risk	If you win	If you lose
You buy 30-year bonds	Interest rate	Capital gain	Capital loss
You buy junk bonds	Default	High interest	Loss of principal ■

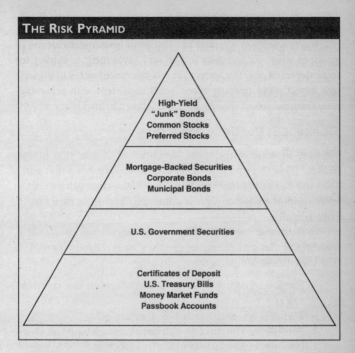

THE RISK PYRAMID

High-Yield
"Junk" Bonds
Common Stocks
Preferred Stocks

Mortgage-Backed Securities
Corporate Bonds
Municipal Bonds

U.S. Government Securities

Certificates of Deposit
U.S. Treasury Bills
Money Market Funds
Passbook Accounts

Stocks. You're betting on the payoff—what the issuing company's performance will be over time. The stock's price can be valued in today's dollars by what the market expects the company to pay each shareholder in the future. That value is based on the company's expected profits. If the profits turn out to be lower or higher than expected, you bought the stock for the wrong price.

In addition, the stock price may be affected by any economic consideration affecting the company, the industry, the region, or the entire stock market. This is referred to as *market risk*. Certain indicators can help you assess to what extent companies will be subject to market risk. One useful concept for this purpose is *beta*. Analysts determine a stock's beta by comparing the stock's historical price changes to that of the market. A stock's beta measures the volatility of its price changes in relation to the stock market's volatility, as represented by the Standard and Poor's 500 Stock Composite Index. A security possessing a beta of 1.0 experiences changes in returns that are approximately equal in proportion and direction to that of the S&P 500. A beta below 1 indicates market risk less than that of the S&P 500, while a beta of greater than 1 indicates market risk above that of the S&P 500.

Concept 3: Portfolio Structure

We have all heard of the adage "don't put all of your eggs in one basket." What this means for asset allocation purposes is that portfolio risk can be reduced by adding asset classes that behave differently from one another. This is commonly known as diversifying your portfolio.

You can use your knowledge of investments and your understanding of risk and return to structure an investment portfolio. The table below compares three portfolios.

- Portfolio A contains only large capitalization U.S. common stocks.
- Portfolio B contains only U.S. Treasury bills.
- Portfolio C contains one-half large capitalization U.S. common stocks and one-half U.S. Treasury bills.

As you might expect—given performance data since 1926—the portfolio containing one-half stock and one-half Treasury bills has an expected return approximately halfway between the two assets' individual expected returns. However, the risk, 10.07%, is lower than halfway between the two assets' individual standard deviations because of the diversification theory described above.

Diversification theory is based on the premise that market values of some assets tend to rise and fall together, whereas the market values of other assets move in opposite directions. Factors independent of the financial characteristics of a particular investment, such as economic, political, and social events, can affect its value. While portfolio risk cannot be totally eliminated, it can be reduced by constructing a diversified portfolio that contains a mix of asset types

COMPARING THREE PORTFOLIOS

	INVESTMENT MIX	EXPECTED RETURN	STANDARD DEVIATION
Portfolio A	100% U.S. Stock	12.52%	20.42%
Portfolio B	100% Treasury Bills	3.77%	3.27%
Portfolio C	50% U.S. Stock 50% Treasury Bills	8.08%	10.07%

whose values have historically moved in opposite directions or in the same direction but to a greater or lesser magnitude.

If you're searching for a particular rate of return, you could combine various assets together to generate this expected return. Many portfolios might provide the same expected return (based on the assets' historical average return), but these portfolios would have different risks. If you're shrewd, you would therefore select the portfolio that meets your return goal but has the lowest possible risk. This is the objective of what is often called *asset allocation*. Asset allocation simply means investing in different types of assets so as to have a diversified portfolio with the highest expected return at a given level of risk. Computer software asset allocation models can help you identify the asset allocation with the highest expected return for a given level of risk.

The following table compares two portfolios with different asset mixes but with the same level of risk (standard deviation).

COMPARING TWO PORTFOLIOS

	PORTFOLIO A	PORTFOLIO B
Treasury Bills	5%	40%
U.S. Stocks	15%	19%
Long-Term Government Bonds	75%	31%
Small Stocks	5%	10%
Portfolio Expected Return	7.13%	7.70%
Portfolio Standard Deviation	8.03%	8.03%

Based on historical data, however, Portfolio B has a higher expected return than Portfolio A. Therefore, if you had a choice of Portfolio A or Portfolio B, you should choose Portfolio B.

The range of risks and returns achievable (based on historical risk and return relationships) are limited by the assets considered in making up the portfolio. Since different assets can have different risk and return characteristics, and since they can behave differently in different economic scenarios, portfolios with higher returns and identical risks may be possible by adding asset classes. For instance, adding international stocks to a portfolio comprised of only U.S. stocks and bonds will reduce risk and increase expected return. This happens because international stocks have historically behaved differently from domestic securities. The diversification effect of international stocks decreases a portfolio's risk (even though international stocks alone can be risky investments). (For a more detailed discussion of international investments, see Chapter 6.)

PLANNER

10 Big Mistakes in Investing — #7
Having too many eggs in one basket

It's important to diversify *among* different investment types (stocks, bonds, cash, international stocks, gold) as well as *within* those asset classes.

STEP 4 | DEVELOP AN INVESTMENT STRATEGY

Once you understand the investment concepts we've discussed, Step 4 is to develop an investment strategy that meets your specific needs. Developing this strategy involves five tasks:

- *Task 1*: Select an asset allocation.
- *Task 2*: Formulate a goal-funding plan.

- *Task 3*: Consider all special opportunities.
- *Task 4*: Understand transaction costs.
- *Task 5*: Weigh the pros and cons of implementation alternatives.

Task 1: Select an Asset Allocation

What asset classes do you want in your portfolio, and in what combination? The asset classes should be as many as possible based on your investment profile. The proportion of your portfolio to allocate to each asset class is ideally determined based on historical data. One way to do this is to use computer software to select a portfolio that meets your target return goal while minimizing your risk. The tables on the following pages show sample asset allocations for young, midlife, pre-retired, and retired investors.

Task 2: Formulate a Goal-Funding Plan

Before you make actual investments, you must identify the specific goals that you want to fund. Then you can purchase the appropriate investments based on when the item being funded will be paid. Therefore, your first task in developing an investment strategy is to formulate a goal-funding plan.

Here are some typical investments suitable for three sample goals:

- *Contingency fund*: money market fund
- *College funding for a 16-year-old*: bonds maturing in 2–6 years
- *College funding for a 2-year-old*: common stock portfolio

Frequently—especially when you're just getting started—your desired long-term asset allocation, based on your risk tolerance and rate of return objectives, won't be possible if you first designate assets to fund your specific goals (e.g., contingency fund, children's college educations, etc.). When this occurs, you may want to focus on funding your short-term goals first; after you've funded those goals, invest in the assets needed to achieve your desired long-term allocation.

ASSET ALLOCATION FOR A YOUNG INVESTOR

Lower Risk

Bonds (30%)

Stocks (35%)

Cash (35%)

Return: 7.3%
After Inflation: 4.1%

Medium Risk

Stocks (55%)

Cash (1%)

Bonds (44%)

Return: 9.3%
After Inflation: 6.1%

Higher Risk

Stocks (75%)

Cash (0%)

Bonds (25%)

Return: 10.7%
After Inflation: 7.5%

ASSET ALLOCATION FOR A MIDLIFE INVESTOR

Lower Risk

Bonds (25%)

Stocks (30%)

Cash (45%)

Return: 6.8%
After Inflation: 3.6%

Medium Risk

Stocks (50%)

Cash (10%)

Bonds (40%)

Return: 8.8%
After Inflation: 5.6%

Higher Risk

Stocks (70%)

Cash (0%)

Bonds (30%)

Return: 10.4%
After Inflation: 7.2%

ASSET ALLOCATION FOR A PRE-RETIRED INVESTOR

Lower Risk

Bonds (21%)   Stocks (25%)

Cash (54%)

Return: 6.3%
After Inflation: 3.1%

Medium Risk

Stocks (45%)

Bonds (36%)   Cash (19%)

Return: 8.3%
After Inflation: 5.1%

Higher Risk

Stocks (65%)

Cash (0%)

Bonds (35%)

Return: 10.0%
After Inflation: 6.8%

ASSET ALLOCATION FOR A RETIRED INVESTOR

Lower Risk

Bonds (25%)   Stocks (30%)

Cash (45%)

Return: 6.8%
After Inflation: 3.6%

Medium Risk

Stocks (40%)

Bonds (33%)   Cash (27%)

Return: 7.8%
After Inflation: 4.6%

Higher Risk

Stocks (60%)

Cash (0%)

Bonds (40%)

Return: 9.6%
After Inflation: 6.4%

Task 3: Consider All Special Opportunities

Part of developing a strategy is to consider the pros and cons of all special opportunities that present themselves. What follows is a brief rundown of some of these opportunities.

Disciplined Savings Opportunities

- Payroll deductions, including deductions for:
  - Credit union
  - U.S. Series EE bonds
  - Employee stock purchase plan
- Automatic transfers from checking account to:
  - Other bank accounts
  - Mutual funds

Tax-Advantaged Vehicles (discussed in Chapter 2)

- 401(k)/403(b) plans
- IRAs
- Keoghs/SEPs
- SIMPLEs

Other Investment Incentives

- Waive service fees if account exceeds particular sums (checking accounts, mutual funds).
- Receive frequent flyer miles for investing in a particular mutual fund.

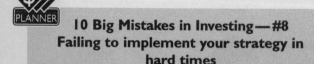

10 Big Mistakes in Investing — #8
Failing to implement your strategy in hard times

If your investment strategy calls for investing in a stock fund every month, do it even if you believe the stock market may decline next month.

Task 4: Understand Transaction Costs

You must also consider the transaction costs involved in investments. Generally, these costs are *commissions* and *income taxes*.

Commissions. Financial intermediaries such as stockbrokers, some mutual funds companies, and banks charge commissions to execute your transactions. Although commissions vary from institution to institution and are based on the type of transaction, they can be negotiated, particularly for large transactions. Commissions on purchases differ from commissions on sales, and the commission percentage will differ for different types of assets as well as for transactions of different sizes. By shopping around, you will be able to compare rates and services that the institutions provide.

Income Taxes. The taxes on investments may also be a significant cost. If you buy a stock for $40 per share and sell it 2 years later for $100 per share, there will generally be a tax on the capital gain at the time of sale. In this case, the gain would be $60 per share, and the federal tax at 20% (the current top tax rate on long-term capital gains) will be $12.00 per share. Most states also impose a tax on capital gains. Thus in this case you will have at most 88% of the asset's value remaining to reinvest. The reinvestment choice must outperform your current stock by a significant amount to make up for the tax cost. Keep in mind, income taxes should *not* be the primary factor in making investment decisions: The decision to retain or sell a particular asset should rest largely on your personal situation, investment goals, and so forth.

Task 5: Weigh the Pros and Cons of Implementation Alternatives

Because you have several different alternatives for implementing your investment strategy, you should carefully weigh the pros and cons of each before proceeding. Perhaps the most significant aspect of your decision is determining what's important to *you* regarding implementation.

Here are some issues that you'll have to face in implementing your strategy. Each involves some trade-offs.

- *Time vs. money.* Do you want to hire someone to look after your investments, or can you do it yourself?
- *Recordkeeping.* Do you want all your investment data on one statement, or are you comfortable with receiving lots of paper documentation? It's easy to underestimate the paperwork involved in tracking individual investments yourself.
- *Income tax planning.* Are you willing to complicate your life to save taxes? For example, an IRA would be yet another account you'd need to keep track of. Are the tax benefits worth the additional paperwork and annual service fees?

5

BUILDING WEALTH THROUGH INVESTMENT PLANNING

- ■ Implement Your Strategy
- ■ Monitor Your Investments

In Chapter 4 we explored Steps 3 and 4 of the investment planning process. Let's now continue with the remaining two steps, in which you:

- Implement your strategy
- Monitor your investments and progress toward reaching your goals

STEP 5   IMPLEMENT YOUR STRATEGY

Once you've decided on an investment portfolio and an appropriate investment strategy, the next step is to implement your investment plan. This involves two fundamental issues: *how to buy* and *when to buy*.

Implementing Your Strategy: *How to Buy*

There are several ways that you can buy investments. Determining the right way for you can be just as important as choosing the investments themselves. In general, you have four options for implementing your plan:

- Through a broker (either full-service or discount)
- Through a professional money manager
- Through a mutual fund
- Through an insurance company

Full-Service Brokers. If you don't have the time, knowledge, experience, or inclination to select securities and manage your portfolio, you should consider a full-service brokerage firm. Full-service brokerage firms provide their customers with a wide variety of services and financial products. If you invest through a full-service brokerage firm, you will receive the firm's research on the economy and particular securities, and periodic newsletters and advice on financial, retirement, and business planning. These firms also offer accounts with check-writing privileges and access to credit cards and other credit facilities. More important, you will receive professional assistance in selecting and managing the securities that are compatible with your investment objectives and goals. Of course, you generally pay for these services and the professional assistance in the form of higher commissions than you would pay if you bought and sold securities yourself through a discount broker.

If you decide to use a full-service firm, make sure that you share your entire financial picture with your broker and articulate your goals and objectives clearly. It is important that your broker understands both what you need and what you expect from him or her.

Discount Brokers. As the name implies, the transaction costs or commissions of a discount broker will generally be lower than the transaction costs at a full-service firm. It is important to remember, however, that although discount brokerage firms can offer a wide array of services, you shouldn't expect to receive personal assistance in the selection and management of the securities in your portfolio. You aren't paying for personal advice—you must decide which investments to purchase or sell. Therefore, using a discount broker is appropriate if you have sufficient time, knowledge, experience, and the inclination to manage your own portfolio.

If you decide that the potential cost savings outweigh the disadvantages, you may want to shop around for your discount broker, since the commission costs and service capabilities of discount brokers can vary dramatically.

Many discount brokers now allow you to invest directly over the Internet with substantial commission savings. Some of these brokers are:

- Brown & Co. (www.brownco.com)
- Charles Schwab (www.eschwab.com)
- Datek (www.datek.com)
- DLJdirect (www.dljdirect.com)
- E*Trade (www.etrade.com)
- Fidelity Web Xpress (www.fidelity.com)

Professional Money Managers. If you have a large sum to invest, you should consider using a professional money manager. Professional money managers have typically distinguished themselves in their profession by way of education, training, and experience in the field of investments.

All money management firms require that you maintain an account at the firm of some minimum size. The minimum size varies from firm to firm. Most firms require an account size of at least $500,000 to $1 million.

However, it is possible to access professional money managers through brokerage firms once your account size is at least $100,000.

Professional money managers charge an annual fee for their services based on a percentage of the assets under their management. A typical annual fee is 1% on the first $1 million under management. In addition, they may also receive the commissions on the buy and sell of securities, depending on whether their firm has the ability to execute the trades.

The advantages of professional asset management are several. First, your portfolio will be individually tailored to meet your personal needs and objectives. You will also receive a high level of personalized services. Most management firms will submit quarterly reports to you that indicate what you own, the activity of your account during the quarter, and most important, how well your portfolio has performed over that quarter and other time periods compared to relevant market indices. Most managers will also meet with you each quarter to discuss your portfolio and their rationale for purchasing or selling specific securities, and to hear from you first-hand any changes in your personal and financial circumstances, and your tax situation.

One important aspect to remember is that the interests of you and the manager are closely aligned. The manager charges a fee based on the value of your portfolio. You want the value of your portfolio to increase and so does the manager. The higher the value of your portfolio, the higher the fee paid to the manager. Because the manager's fee is determined primarily by the value of your portfolio, there is no apparent incentive for the manger to trade the securities in your portfolio excessively in order to earn commissions.

Owning Mutual Funds. One alternative to purchasing individual securities outright is owning mutual funds. A mutual fund is an investment company that invests in cash, bonds, stocks, or other investments. The purchasers of the fund's shares essentially each own a portion of each investment owned by the fund.

For diversification purposes, mutual funds can be an appropriate investment vehicle for small to medium-sized portfolios. If you can't afford to purchase 100 shares of 30 different stocks, you may be able to afford 100 shares of a mutual fund that invests in those same 30 stocks. Your funds are pooled with many other investors, thereby enabling the pool to invest in more securities than might otherwise be feasible.

An additional advantage: The firms that manage the mutual fund, as well as the person who is responsible for investing the money, are professionals. Although you, your stockbroker, or your financial planner must research the mutual fund, you do not have to research every asset it holds.

Because mutual funds are important investments, we explore this subject in more detail in the next chapter.

Investing in Annuities. An annuity is a contract between you—the annuitant—and an insurance company. You invest in the contract and receive a promise from the insurance company to pay a series of payments for a fixed number of years or over your lifetime. The payments can begin immediately or can be delayed to a future date.

The primary advantage of a tax-deferred annuity is that the investment earnings remain tax-deferred until the funds are withdrawn. With certain exceptions, any earnings withdrawn prior to age 59½ are generally subject to a 10% penalty for early withdrawal in addition to ordinary income taxes. (See both *The Ernst & Young Tax Guide* and *The Ernst & Young Tax Saver's Guide*, published annually by John Wiley & Sons, Inc., for details of these early withdrawal penalties.) In this regard, annuities operate similarly to IRAs. However, unlike IRAs, you aren't limited in the amount of money you can place in a tax-deferred annuity.

There are two kinds of annuities: *immediate* and *deferred*.

- *Immediate annuities*. With an immediate annuity you invest in the annuity and your payments start immediately.
- *Deferred annuities*. With a deferred annuity you pay your premium and payments don't start until more than a year later. Deferred annuities constitute the bigger segment of the market by far. The reason for their popularity is that the annuity's buildup, like that of an IRA, is tax-deferred until withdrawn.

Deferred annuities themselves come in two types. One is the *fixed annuity*, which functions like a CD in a tax-sheltered wrapper. Your account is credited with a fixed interest rate that the company can change at fixed intervals (usually once a year). By contrast, the *variable annuity* has mutual fund clones within it—separate funds in which you can put your money. You can then transfer to different mutual funds within the annuity. Variable annuities are quite popular because they allow both free deferral of investment income and the ability to diversify among several types of funds. With current high tax rates, the attraction is obvious.

BUILDER   If you're considering a fixed annuity, you need to investigate these issues for each product:

- The company's financial strength, and thus its ability to invest and safeguard your money
- The product's specific features, including:
  - Its surrender charges
  - The conditions under which you can withdraw money without a surrender charge
  - The conditions under which you can bail out of the policy penalty-free if it doesn't meet certain criteria
- The company's crediting history (i.e., have they consistently paid reasonable rates to annuity holders over the years?)

For a variable annuity, you should consider these issues:

- How good are the investment choices?
- What are the track records for those funds?
- What are the features of that particular annuity?
  - Are you able to move money around easily?
  - Is there an 800 number to call, or do you have to make changes through your broker?
- How high are the annual charges?

What makes one annuity better than another? It depends on whether your primary desire is a pre-determined rate of return (fixed) or tax-advantaged investments (variable).

Is an annuity right for you? Perhaps—if you can wait long enough for the annuity's compounding to offset the additional charges as well as phase out the back-end load. People who have sufficient liquidity and investable assets outside their retirement plan are good candidates for annuities. Other candidates are people who feel sure they will be in the same or a lower bracket at the time of retirement. Under those circumstances, an annuity can be a useful vehicle. However, you should have enough liquidity outside the annuity so that you can leave your money in the annuity for the required timespan, at least to avoid a back-end load.

Implementing Your Strategy: *When to Buy*

We've explored the various means to investing; now for the issue of timing your investments. Frequently, investors will try to time their investment decisions according to whether they believe a particular market is over- or undervalued. For example, if you think the stock market is overvalued, you may decide to wait until it declines before making additional stock market investments. You may even reduce your current stock market holdings, reasoning that you'll increase them again once the market has bottomed out after its "inevitable" decline.

The flaw in this strategy is that it's very difficult for individual investors to forecast accurately when financial markets will rise or fall. Any information that an individual investor has is almost certainly already known by investment professionals and is therefore already reflected in the market's value. The most experienced investment analysts who track financial markets daily cannot predict market swings with much accuracy—are you likely to outdo them?

Based on historical market data, it appears that an asset allocation should be strategic and long-term rather than one that you change frequently depending on your forecast of the markets. Most investment advisors agree that you have a much better chance of reaching your goals if you have a long-term investment perspective.

10 Big Mistakes in Investing — #9 Timing the market

It doesn't work—the opportunity cost of investing in cash investments tends to exceed market losses over time.

Since it's impossible to predict consistently whether the market is high or low, the problem is to invest at the right time without resorting to market timing techniques. For example, if you invested $20,000 in the stock market on one day and the next day the market lost 20% of its value, you will wish that you had waited an extra day before you invested.

One method of investing that addresses this concern is *dollar cost averaging*. Here's an example. Let's say that you have $2,500 to invest. Using dollar cost averaging, as shown in the table below, you'd not invest all your money at once; instead, you'd invest (for example) $500 per month for 5 months. When the stock's price is low, this $500 purchases more shares; when the price is high, it purchases fewer shares. While the average price of the asset over the 5 months is $4.10 ($20.50/5), the average cost you've paid is only $3.85 ($2,500/650). By being disciplined and not investing more money when the price *seems* low or less money when the price *seems* high, you've managed to get neither the best price nor the worst price. But what you have achieved is an average cost that is lower than the

DOLLAR COST AVERAGING

Month	Price per share	Dollars invested	Number of shares
1	$ 5.00	$ 500	100
2	4.00	500	125
3	2.50	500	200
4	4.00	500	125
5	5.00	500	100
Total	**$20.50**	**$2,500**	**650**

average price. Note that the time period over which you invest the money can span several months (as shown here), several quarters, or even several years, depending on how much money you have available to invest and what your preferences are. Moreover, committing your savings to the market at predetermined intervals enables you to take advantage of dollar cost averaging continuously.

STEP 6	# MONITOR YOUR INVESTMENTS AND PROGRESS TOWARD REACHING YOUR GOALS

Once you've implemented your investment strategy, it's important that you monitor your investments from time to time to ensure that they remain appropriate for your financial goals. While you should generally try to avoid frequent changes to your investments, you should periodically assess each investment's performance to see that it meets your expectations. A long-term investor generally shouldn't make new investment decisions based on a one-year return, but it's important for you to understand why a particular investment outperformed or underperformed expectations.

When evaluating your investments' performance, you should consider the financial environment in which the performance occurred. One cause for underperformance of an investment or a money manager may be the financial markets in general. You should always consider your investments' performance in relation to the appropriate benchmarks. For example, you might want to compare your U.S. stock portfolio's returns to the S&P 500, and your international stock portfolio's performance to the EAFE (Europe/ Australia/Far East) index.

Just as you must consider risk as well as return when selecting investments, you must also consider risk when evaluating your investments' performance. If your money manager or mutual fund takes on more risk than the market itself does, the return should also exceed that of the market over the long term.

E
X
A
M
P
L
E
■ Let's suppose that the S&P 500's return was 10% and your U.S. stock mutual fund's return was 10.5%. Should you be pleased? The answer: It depends. Comparing these returns without making an adjustment for risk prevents you from comparing apples to apples. ■

To understand how your investment performed, given its risk, you need to adjust the return to account for the risk difference. *Beta*—described in Chapter 4—is often used to make this adjustment. If your mutual fund's beta is 1.10, your mutual fund manager may have taken on 10% more risk than the market. Therefore if the return is not 10% greater than the market's return, the performance may be lower than the market's on a risk-adjusted basis, even though its nominal return is higher.

The measurement that compares returns on a risk-adjusted basis is *alpha*. If alpha is a positive number, it means that the investment portfolio performed better than expected, given the risk of the portfolio. The higher the alpha, the better the risk-adjusted performance has been. A negative alpha indicates underperformance, given the portfolio's presumed risk.

Another important factor: In reevaluating your investment plan, you should consider whether your investment objectives have changed due to a change in your personal or financial circumstances. Changes in your income tax rate, portfolio size, or risk tolerance may affect your investment strategy as well. Finally, because financial markets are continually evolving, the spectrum of investment vehicles available may expand over time, offering you new choices that may fit your investment goals more precisely.

SUMMARY

It takes careful planning, discipline, and diligence to achieve your financial goals. The wide variety of investment products available, the increasing complexity and globalization of financial markets, and the changing income tax laws mean that you should make use of all available resources to succeed in today's investment environment.

To begin your investment planning process, you must ask yourself the following questions:

- Specifically, what are my financial goals?
- Considering my existing investments, future savings, and time horizon, what investment return must I achieve to meet these goals?

These questions will prompt you to evaluate your current financial situation and use financial projections to determine how you can achieve your goals.

Once you have answered the questions posed above, you should ask:

- What characteristics am I looking for in an investment to help me meet my goals?
- Considering the array of investment products available to me, which classes of investments match my investment objectives?

After studying financial markets and researching investments, your next steps are to:

- Determine what mix of asset classes might allow you to achieve the return you need while taking the minimum risk.
- Consider whether you have sufficient cash to meet your short-term needs and unexpected emergencies.
- Decide which assets are appropriate inside your retirement plans and which to invest elsewhere. (See Chapter 6 for further information.)

To implement your investment plan, you must then decide whether to purchase individual securities through a broker, use mutual funds or tax-deferred annuities, or employ a professional money manger. Once your investment plan is in place, you should periodically:

- Monitor the performance of your investments.
- Reevaluate your financial goals and investment objectives.
- Reassess financial markets and the investments available to you.
- Make changes in your investment plan as necessary.

6

BUILDING WEALTH (CONCLUDED)

Through the preceding four chapters, we've worked our way systematically through the investment planning process. Here, now, are discussions of five issues that overlap with one or more aspects of investing:

- Mutual funds
- Foreign investments
- Real estate
- Gold
- Investing for retirement

MUTUAL FUNDS

In Chapter 5 we briefly mentioned mutual funds as a method for investment. Mutual funds are, in fact, one of the most appropriate means of investing for many people.

Successful investing requires time, effort, and knowledge. You have to spend time identifying your objectives and designing an investment strategy to meet them. However, you don't necessarily need to spend the considerable amount of time and energy required to search for investment opportunities and to monitor the investments you select. Instead, you can have a professional investment manager assist you in implementing your investment strategy. As we noted earlier, however, a personal investment manager can be inaccessible unless you have at least $500,000 to invest—and many managers won't even consider a client with investments of less than $1 million.

Does this mean that you're entirely on your own? Not at all. You can receive professional investment management through *regulated investment companies* such as mutual funds or unit investment trusts. These investment companies don't provide you with a portfolio designed for you individually. Instead, you own an interest in the entire pool of investments managed by the professional investment manager.

Regulated investment companies are firms that receive funds from many investors, pool the funds, and use them to purchase investments that the companies' professional investment managers select. Since the investor owns shares in the investment company, he or she owns a share of its portfolio of investments. Regulated investment companies are commonly referred to as *mutual funds*.

The advantages that investment companies can offer you are numerous, including:

- Professional investment management of assets at a relatively low cost
- Ownership in a diversified portfolio
- Potentially lower commissions, since the investment company buys and sells in large blocks
- Prospectuses and reports of various periodicals to assist people in readily accessing information needed to perform fund comparisons
- Other special services, such as dividend reinvestment plans, periodic withdrawal and investment plans, telephone switching, and in some cases, check writing

Q: Where can I find information about mutual funds?

A: Try these sources:

Morningstar Mutual Funds. An exhaustive compendium of mutual fund data on over 1,300 funds. Updated every other week. Price: about $400 per year or $5 per page on individual funds. Source: Morningstar, Inc., 225 West Wacker Drive, Suite 400, Chicago, IL 60606. Phone: (800) 876-5005.

Directory of Mutual Funds. Data on approximately 3,000 funds. No performance information. Updated annually. Price: about $10. Source: Investment Company Institute, 1401 H Street, NW, Suite 1200, Washington, DC 20005. Phone: (202) 326-5800.

Investor's Guide to Low-Cost Mutual Funds. Detailed information about 750 no-load and low-load funds; updated twice annually. Price: $5.00. Source: Mutual Fund Education Alliance, 1900 Erie Street, Suite 120, Kansas City, MO 64116. Phone: (816) 471-1454.

Individual Investor's Guide to Low-Load Mutual Funds. In-depth analysis of over 800 funds; updated annually. Price: about $25. Source: American Association of Individual Investors, 625 North Michigan Avenue, Suite 1900, Chicago, IL 60611. Phone: (312) 280-0170.

The Value Line Mutual Fund Survey. Data on approximately 1,500 established funds and 500 newer funds. Updated three times per year. Price: about $300 per year. Source: The Value Line Mutual Fund Survey, Dept. 6708, 220 East 42nd Street, New York, NY 10017. Phone: (800) 284-7607, ext. 6708.

Standard & Poor's/Lipper Mutual Fund Profiles. Data on approximately 750 funds; updated quarterly. Price: about $150 per year. Source: Standard & Poor's, 25 Broadway, Suite 1900, New York, NY 10004. Phone: (800) 221-5277.

And these online sources:

- www.mfea.com/educidx.html
- www.fundfinder.com

- www.fundfocus.com
- www.quicken.com/investments/mutualfunds/finder

Investment Objectives

Mutual funds are classified according to their investment objectives. Following is a summary of the various types of funds categorized by their investment objective.

Aggressive Growth Funds. These funds are characterized by high risk and high return: They typically seek capital appreciation and do not produce significant interest income or dividends.

Growth Funds. Growth funds aim to achieve an increase in the value of their investments over the long term (capital gains) rather than paying dividends.

Growth and Income Funds. Also called "equity-income" and "total return" funds, these funds aim to balance the objectives of long-term growth and current income.

Balanced Funds. These funds have three objectives: to conserve investors' initial principal, to pay high current income through dividends and interest, and to promote long-term growth of both principal and income. Balanced funds invest in both bonds and stocks.

Bond Funds. Bond mutual funds invest primarily in bonds. Some funds may concentrate on short-term bonds, others on intermediate-term bonds, and still others on long-term bonds.

Sector Funds. Sector funds invest in one industry, such as biotechnology or retail, and therefore do not offer the diversity you generally receive from a growth mutual fund, for example.

Index Funds. Index mutual funds recreate a particular market index (e.g., the S&P 500). The holdings and the return should mirror that of the index.

Types of Regulated Investment Companies

In addition to categorizing investment companies by their investment objectives, investment companies are classified according to their capital structure. The three types are:

- Closed-end funds
- Unit investment trusts
- Open-end funds

Closed-End Funds. Closed-end investment companies have a set capital structure with a specified number of shares. For this reason, investors must generally purchase existing shares of closed-end funds from current stockholders. Investors who wish to liquidate their position in closed-end investment companies must sell their shares to other investors. Shares in closed-end funds are therefore traded on the open market just like the stock of publicly held corporations. As a result, closed-end funds have an additional risk that isn't present in open-end funds—their price does not necessarily equal their net asset value. Closed-end funds that are sold at a discount from the value of the underlying investments can produce an opportunity for greater return.

 What happens if my mutual fund company goes broke? Do I lose my investment?

 No. The mutual fund company only *manages* the investments held by the fund.

Unit Investment Trusts. Unit investment trusts are a variation of closed-end funds. Unit trusts typically invest in a fixed portfolio of bonds that are held until maturity rather than managed and traded, as is the case with bond mutual funds. As an investor you purchase units that represent an ownership in the trust assets. Because the bonds are not traded, the annual fees charged for unit trusts may be lower than those charged by bond mutual funds. The unit trust collects the interest income and repayment of principal of the bonds held in the portfolio and distributes these funds to the unit holders. Unit investment trusts can provide you with a portfolio of bonds that have different maturity dates and an average holding period that meets your objectives. Cash flow is relatively predictable, since the intention is to hold the bonds until maturity.

Open-End Funds. Commonly referred to as mutual funds, open-end funds differ from closed-end funds in that they do not have a fixed number of shares to issue. Instead, the number of shares outstanding varies as investors purchase and redeem them directly from the open-end investment company. An investor who wants a position in a particular mutual fund purchases the shares from the fund either through a stockbroker or by contacting the fund directly. Conversely, mutual fund shareholders who want to liquidate their position sell their shares back to the company. The value of a share in a mutual fund is determined by the net asset value (NAV). Funds compute NAV by dividing the value of the fund's total net assets by the number of shares outstanding.

Mutual Funds Fees

The costs associated with open-end fund shares resemble those for closed-end funds. Like closed-end funds, open-end funds bear the trading costs and investment management fees of the investment company. However, mutual fund investors may or may not be subject to a sales charge referred to as a "load."

Depending on the type of load charged (if any), open-end mutual funds are classified as:

- No-load funds
- 12b-1 funds
- Load funds

No-Load Funds. No-load funds don't impose a sales charge on their investors. Purchases and sales of shares in a no-load fund are made at the fund's NAV per share. Consequently, every dollar invested gets allocated to the fund for investment rather than having a portion permanently kept back to cover sales charges.

12b-1 Funds. 12b-1 funds are a variation on no-load funds. While every dollar paid into the fund is committed to investment, the 12b-1 fund shareholders indirectly pay an annual fee to cover the fund's sales and marketing costs. This 12b-1 fee typically ranges from 0.1% to the maximum 1% of total fund assets. [*Note*: The 12b-1 fee is assessed every year (instead of only once); thus the longer you hold your 12b-1 fund shares, the greater the sales charge you will bear.]

Load Funds. By contrast, load funds charge the shareholder a direct commission at the time of purchase and/or when the shares are redeemed. "Front-end loads" are charged to the investor at the time of purchase and can be as high as 8.5% of the gross amount invested. On the other hand, some load funds charge their share-holders the load at the time their shares are redeemed. This cost will be either a "back-end load" or a "redemption fee." A back-end load is based on the lesser of the initial cost or final value of the shares redeemed and may disappear after a few years. A redemp-tion fee is similar to a back-end load, but is based on the value of the shares you choose to redeem rather than your initial invest-ment. It typically applies if the investor sells within a very short period of time (usually 30 to 60 days). The purpose of such fees is to discourage shareholders from short-term trading of fund shares.

All fees, loads, and charges reduce your investment return. Therefore, you should consider not only a fund's return, but all of the expenses that affect this return.

Mutual Fund Literature

Fund literature produced by the mutual fund company managing the fund is generally readily available. It will provide you with im-portant information, such as what expenses a fund assesses. The Securities and Exchange Commission (SEC) has imposed minimum uniform reporting requirements on these companies to facilitate consumer comparison of funds.

Prospectus. The prospectus is the most important document that the fund provides. In fact, you are required to sign a statement stating that you've read this document and that you're familiar with its contents before you can purchase fund shares. The SEC has standardized the content and format of mutual fund prospectuses. All prospectuses now include a fee table listing all its expenses. The table also gives the fund's return, net of these expenses, for 1, 2, 3, 5, and 10 years, assuming a $1,000 initial investment and a 5% annual growth rate. This lets you compare apples to apples.

Prospectuses also include condensed financial information providing statistics of income and capital changes per share in the fund. Among the most useful data are the following:

- *The net investment income line* enables you to determine the level and stability of net income over the time period analyzed.
- *The annual net asset value amounts* help you trace the change in value per share from year to year.
- *The ratio of expenses to average net assets* helps you compare the funds' expense ratio.
- *The portfolio turnover rate* indicates how many times the value of all holdings have been sold, allowing you to assess trading costs.

The prospectus also gives you the fund's investment objectives and policies. The fund's objectives and attitudes toward risk should coincide with your objectives and risk tolerance.

Statement of Additional Information. Another SEC-required document is the "Statement of Additional Information." Sometimes included in the prospectus, this statement elaborates on the fund's investment objectives, restrictions, board of directors, and tax consequences of fund distributions.

Portfolio Manager. One important item that you usually *don't* find in the prospectus or other literature provided by the mutual fund company is the portfolio manager's name and tenure. The portfolio manager works for the fund and is responsible for the fund's daily investment activities. For some funds more than others, it may be important to make sure that the person who achieved the returns you initially found impressive is still employed by the fund. You can typically call the fund and request this person's name and experience.

Account Statements. Account statements track your reinvested dividend and capital gains distributions, purchases, redemptions, and fees. You should save these statements for tax purposes. You are taxed on dividends and capital gains as you earn them, even if you reinvest them. Therefore, you will also receive a 1099-B and 1099-DIV in January of each year for the prior year's distributions. The amount of any reinvested distributions is added to the cost basis of your mutual fund shares.

Mutual Fund Application Form

When completing a mutual fund application form, you have the opportunity to make elections that will facilitate managing the account. For example, you will be asked whether you want to receive your distributions in cash or have them reinvested in your account. Electing the reinvestment option prevents your having to reinvest the funds, since they are reinvested for you automatically. Reinvestment is similar to dollar cost averaging, since your distributions will buy shares each payment date.

Other elections include:

- *Wire transfer of distributions* to your regular bank account
- *Transfer of funds* directly from your checking account to your mutual fund account
- *Telephone redemption of shares*

All of these services can facilitate fund transfers and reduce your time commitment and paperwork.

10 Big Mistakes in Investing — #10 Paying income tax on someone else's capital gain

Most mutual funds charge their shareholders of record on a particular date in December with their proportionate share of all the capital gains that the funds have realized from selling assets all year. The result: You gain immediate taxable income without increasing your shares' value. To avoid this problem, find out when the fund posts its gains for the year; then buy your shares after that date.

FOREIGN INVESTMENTS

Investment professionals in this country are of two minds about foreign investments. Some argue that foreign investing can result in greater overall portfolio returns, given the advantages of diversifying among investments and taking advantage of differing economic scenarios worldwide. (See the diversification discussion in Chapter 4.) Other successful investment managers advocate investing only in domestic enterprises: They believe that given American companies' foreign operations or foreign sales, domestic stocks provide the needed foreign exposure. Certainly, the incremental return on any foreign investment must be large enough to compensate for the applicable foreign exchange risk.

> **Foreign exchange risk:** the risk that a foreign currency will depreciate in relation to the U.S. dollar, thus diminishing the dollar value of the foreign investment.

If you decide to diversify your portfolio internationally, you have several ways to implement your choices.

- Direct foreign stock purchases
- American depository receipts (ADRs)
- Stock mutual funds
- Foreign stock mutual funds
- Foreign bond mutual funds
- Foreign currency accounts
- U.S. bonds denominated in foreign currencies

Direct Foreign Stock Purchases

If you have timely access to foreign information, a desire to keep abreast of the international market, and lots of time, you might consider investing directly in foreign stocks. A caveat, however: This course of action requires a relatively large amount of investment capital, may be complicated, and can be expensive.

American Depository Receipts (ADRs)

ADRs are dollar-denominated negotiable receipts that represent the stock of a foreign company. This stock is held by foreign branches of U.S. banks. These receipts are listed on one of the major U.S. stock exchanges and represent an alternative to direct investing. As with direct foreign stock purchases, be sure you have adequate information to evaluate the foreign company and the market in which it operates.

Stock Mutual Funds

Many stock mutual funds invest in foreign stocks. In 1994, for instance, Fidelity Magellan had approximately 10% invested in foreign stocks. Thus you may get foreign exposure even in a mutual fund that isn't technically a foreign mutual fund.

Foreign Stock Mutual Funds

Hundreds of mutual funds exist that allow American investors to share in a piece of the international investing pie. Fund managers handle the investment research and selection process for their investors. They trade securities daily, seeking potentially favorable opportunities while hedging against unfavorable movements in interest rates and currency exchange rates. Mutual funds in this market go by many names but can be divided into the following categories:

- *Global or world funds.* These funds invest anywhere in the world, including the United States.
- *International or foreign funds.* Such funds invest anywhere in the world except the United States.
- *Regional funds.* These invest in specific geographic areas, such as Europe, Latin America, or the Pacific Rim.
- *Country funds.* Funds of this sort invest entirely in a specific country. For the most part, single country funds are closed-end mutual funds that typically trade on either the New York Stock Exchange or the American Stock Exchange.
- *International index funds.* These are mutual funds that parallel the concept of a domestic equity index fund. They are designed and operated so that their portfolios mirror the composition of the market index after which the funds are named.

Foreign Bond Mutual Funds

In addition to foreign stock funds, numerous foreign bond funds are available for investment. Since economic conditions differ from country to country, interest rates vary as well. At any given time, you can usually find several countries with interest rates higher than those in the United States. There is a downside to consider, though. Overseas interest rates may be more attractive, but language barriers, differing regulations, and illiquid markets all increase the challenge of foreign investments. Fluctuating currency values, although a potential advantage, can work against you if the currency of your foreign investment loses value relative to the U.S. dollar.

The emphasis on stable share prices is strongest with short-term global income funds. Short maturities help lessen the effect of interest rate fluctuations on asset values. This helps keep share-price volatility low, thereby allowing you to take advantage of worldwide, short-term interest rates with relatively low risk to principal. If you prefer a more aggressive approach, consider global income funds that invest in longer-term debt securities. The interest rate risk increases with longer maturities, but opportunities for higher returns increase as well.

Foreign Currency Accounts

Larger U.S. banking institutions offer deposit accounts through which you may invest in foreign currencies. The types of accounts, minimum investments, and currency selections vary. Foreign currency accounts let you take advantage of foreign interest rates at times when they are superior to domestic money market and CD rates, and they allow you to benefit from currency rate fluctuations. Furthermore, your deposits are insured by the Federal Deposit Insurance Corporation (FDIC) for up to $100,000. A caveat, however: The FDIC doesn't insure against loss of principal due to unfavorable exchange rates.

U.S. Bonds Denominated in Foreign Currencies

These investments offer the familiarity and safety of a U.S. issuer coupled with the opportunity to benefit from foreign currency fluctuations. During the 1980s, U.S. government agencies (such as the Student Loan Marketing Association and the Federal Home Loan Bank) offered several foreign currency issues that are traded in U.S. markets. In addition, several major domestic corporations offer bonds denominated in foreign currencies. They are available in varying maturities, yields, and currency assignments. Upon maturity, the face value will be paid in the listed currency, such as the Japanese yen or the British pound. Depending on the currency exchange rate at maturity, you may realize gain or loss on the currency transaction.

REAL ESTATE

Real estate has long been popular, for more reasons than investment alone. Fully 60% of Americans own their own homes, and many do so for reasons that go beyond considerations of financial planning. There's an intrinsic satisfaction in owning your own property. Small wonder that many people regard home ownership as part of their concept of the American Dream.

Ownership

You can own real estate either directly or indirectly. Direct ownership involves purchasing particular properties (e.g., your home or a duplex). Indirect ownership involves investing money in a partnership or trust that owns one or more pieces of real estate. The pros and cons of the direct vs. indirect ownership of real estate are shown in the table below.

Direct Ownership	Indirect Ownership
You can pick the property	Someone else picks the property
Ability to find a good deal	Greater diversification opportunities (geographic and type of real estate)
Possible tax advantages	Reduced tax advantages (but still able to offset net rental income with deferral)
Complicates tax return (you must learn depreciation and other rules about tax deductions)	Complicates tax return (you must wait to receive the K-1 to be able to prepare your return and learn complicated tax rules)
Control	Professional management
Greater cash requirements and cash flow risk	Lower cash commitment and limited liability

Kinds of Real Estate Investment

Direct ownership is the most common method of investing in real estate, dominated by ownership of primary residences. Ownership of vacation homes or rental properties are the second-most-common arrangements. Indirect ownership is accomplished primarily through limited partnerships and real estate investment trusts (REITs).

Home Ownership. Many people have found that home ownership has provided an investment return as well as a physical shelter. The investment return comes from your home's increase in value while you own it. This so-called investment return, however, cannot be realized in the form of cash until the homeowner is ready to "trade down." The main drawbacks of direct ownership are the amount of time spent in managing the property, and possible uninsured risks.

PLANNER Have you considered buying a vacation home as an investment? Sometimes it works out well—but look before you leap. It's not always the care-free haven you imagine. First, consider the costs you'd never have to think about regarding non-real estate investments, including:

- Furniture and decorating
- Home maintenance
- Landscaping or upkeep of the yard
- Utilities
- Security

There are also other, nonfinancial demands the property will make on you. Once you buy the place, you'll feel you have to spend all your vacations there. You want to get your money's worth, right? Perhaps you like the area so much you're always happy to be there. On the other hand, many people find a vacation home more work than they thought. What are the odds, for instance, that you'll spend most of your "off time" doing household projects?

Another possibility is that you bought the vacation home as a future retirement home. This may well suit your purposes. The leverage benefits of real estate can make buying this sort of property in advance advantageous. However, consider these other issues as well:

- Are you sure that the home is located where you want to retire?
- How near will your friends and family be to the home?
- Will owning the home limit your options for travel elsewhere?

Rental Property. Rental property can be a source of a current income stream—and due to available depreciation deductions, often a tax-deferred income stream at that. In addition, rental property (as is also true for personal residences) has historically provided investors with an inflation hedge and potential for capital appreciation. You should consider the potential disadvantages of rental arrangements, however:

- The tax rules for deducting out-of-pocket expenses and depreciation are complicated. (See *The Ernst & Young Tax Guide*, published annually by John Wiley & Sons, Inc., for more details.)
- Demands on your time for upkeep and paperwork may be burdensome.
- Ownership may limit your mobility under some circumstances.

> *Depreciation deduction: a tax deduction or write-off of the cost of an asset over its estimated useful life.*

Limited Partnership Interests. A limited partnership interest can provide passive participation in real estate in two characteristic situations: (1) for larger properties, and (2) where direct investor management isn't desired or practical. Unlike a corporation, a partnership itself is not subject to tax. Instead, the partnership's items of income and deduction flow through to and are reported on the tax returns of the individual partners. This will complicate your preparation of tax returns, since you must wait to receive a Schedule K-1 from the partnership before you can finish your return. (Even when you finally receive it, you may find it so confusing that you'll have to hire an accountant to help you make sense of it.) Limited partners do not have a voice in the management of the partnership but have liability limited to their investment in the partnership.

> **Limited partnership interest:** *an interest in an investment in which the investor's liability is solely the investment and the limited partner is not involved in the administration of the partnership.*

Real Estate Investment Trusts (REITs). REITs are publicly traded entities that invest in real estate. Their operations are similar to those of mutual funds. REITs generally invest in income-producing properties and/or mortgages and pass the income and capital gains through to investors. Advantages of REITs include professional and centralized management, greater liquidity, and diversification. However, REITs (unlike limited partnerships) cannot pass through losses.

The Ups and Downs of Real Estate

When evaluating property for investment, you need to look at its real growth potential, not just its ability to act as an inflation hedge. During the 1970s, making money in real estate was easy, but a great deal of the increase in property values resulted from inflation and not necessarily from real growth. Although real estate is often an excellent hedge against inflation, there are risks associated with any real estate investment. The *location and age of the property* and the *general economic conditions* may affect both its income and appreciation potential. *Triple net leases*—in which the tenant is responsible for the costs of maintenance, insurance, and taxes—may offer less risk than leases in which the lessor is responsible for these costs. Also, the extent to which *debt or leverage* is used can magnify the potential upside and downside of a real estate investment.

Due to these many risks, a diversified portfolio of real estate is a safer investment vehicle than an investment in a single piece of property. Some limited partnerships and REITs own many properties in different locations, thus allowing for diversification.

Another attribute of real estate is *illiquidity*. Unlike a U.S. Treasury note or common stock, real estate cannot quickly be turned into cash at its fair market value. It takes time for a transaction to close. Also, if you hold the real estate in a limited partnership, your limited partnership interests aren't readily salable.

Tax Issues and Real Estate

In the past, many people relied on depreciation expenses and the deductibility of tax losses to improve the rate of return on their real estate investments. Now, not only have depreciation deductions been reduced; if operating expenses exceed operating income, the net cash loss may no longer be offset by tax savings. Losses from rented real estate are generally considered passive losses. For this reason, they can be used only to reduce passive income, not income from other sources (such as compensation, interest, or dividends). There is an exception if you actively participate in the real estate activity under which a maximum of $25,000 in losses may be currently deductible if your adjusted gross income is under $100,000.

> **Active participation:** *participating in ways that include management decisions or arranging for others to provide services.*

Before you invest in real estate, you should therefore consider the possibility that any operating or tax losses incurred may not be deductible currently, although unused "suspended" losses can generally be used when you sell the property. A thorough reading of the pertinent sections of *The Ernst & Young Tax Guide* and *The Ernst & Young Tax Savers Guide* should be your first step.

In addition to potential tax benefits and diversification advantages, real estate can provide you with leverage.

Leverage. Leverage means that you can purchase an asset with debt as well as some cash. The greater the debt, the higher the leverage. High leverage results in an ability to magnify your investment returns as well as your risk.

Here's an example of leverage at work in a real estate investment. Let's say that you've invested $10,000 cash and borrowed $40,000 and now own a $50,000 real estate investment. If the value of the property increases 10% or $5,000, the return on your cash investment is 50%, not 10%.

Although you can leverage with stocks, you can leverage even more with real estate. The most you can leverage stocks is generally 50%; by contrast, you can put down only 20% on a real estate investment resulting in much greater leverage.

GOLD

To protect against inflation and to diversify your portfolio, some investment professionals would recommend allocating a small percentage of your funds to gold and other precious metals. Historically, gold has provided a hedge against falling stock prices, since it tends to behave in a manner opposite to that of stocks in most economic scenarios. Gold and other precious metals are therefore significant investments from a diversification standpoint.

 Q: The value of gold has risen dramatically during past global crises. Is this likely to happen at such times in the future?

 A: Historically, gold has behaved in a manner opposite to stocks' performance. When there's a financial or political crisis, some investors abandon stocks for a tangible asset which they feel will always have value. Whether this will happen in the future remains uncertain.

A final consideration: Owning gold involves costs atypical of other investments. These costs include:

- Assaying
- Storage
- Illiquidity
- Insurance

> **Assaying:** examination and determination as to certain characteristics, such as weight, measure, or quality.

An alternative to owning gold outright is investing in companies in that industry. You could do so by purchasing individual stocks or by purchasing shares in a mutual fund that invests in gold stocks or precious metals.

INVESTING FOR RETIREMENT

Finally, let's touch on another topic that overlaps with the general discussions so far but also involves its own specific issues. This topic is investing for retirement.

There are two schools of thought regarding which investments to select with the money inside your retirement plans. One school says that you should invest in stocks; the other bonds.

The Case for Stocks

In setting up a retirement plan, you're putting in assets today that you don't intend to use until you reach your 60s and beyond. Consequently, the assets being invested to meet your retirement goals probably have the longest *investment horizon* relative to the other assets in your portfolio. The longer your time horizon, the more risk you can tolerate. Therefore, the argument goes, your retirement plan assets should be invested in the riskiest types of investments in your portfolio. This generally means stocks.

The Case for Bonds

The primary investment advantage of funds placed in an IRA or other retirement plan is their tax-deferred compounding of earnings. For this reason, the counterargument goes that it is generally appropriate to invest in assets that ordinarily produce a lot of current income each year—that is, bonds.

Stocks or Bonds?

Capital losses are generally allowed up to $3,000 annually, although those realized inside an IRA or other retirement plan are not deductible. In addition, net capital gains are taxed at lower rates if realized outside an IRA, and that tax is deferred until the time of sale for assets held outside an IRA. All distributions from IRAs and other retirement plans are taxed at the higher ordinary income tax rates, albeit with the tax deferred until the funds are distributed. Thus you may be better off holding lower-yielding, growth-oriented investments such as stocks outside IRAs and retirement plans to take advantage of their benefits, while investing in higher-yielding investments such as bonds inside retirement plans. If you invest in a Roth IRA, however, these investment principles may differ since the income from a Roth IRA is tax free.

Whichever approach you select, remember to make sure that you're achieving your overall asset allocation when you're investing your retirement plan assets. Let's look at investment strategies specific to 401(k) plans and IRAs.

401(k) Plans. Often, 401(k) plans offer several investment choices. Many people choose to invest their 401(k) plan assets in some or all of the investment choices, based on their desired asset allocation. Some employers assist employees in selecting this mix by providing them with sample asset allocations, based on the historical risk and return of the available investment choices.

Most 401(k) plans also offer a guaranteed investment contract (GIC) as an investment. The reason? GICs often provide a higher rate of return than other cash-type investments. GICs are not risk-free. However, they may have a valid role to play in the retirement planning portion of a diversified portfolio. There are situations in which GICs make sense, since they are generally more predictable than stocks, and they generally offer interest comparable to that of a long-term bond. For example, you may need to focus on preserving capital if you're nearing retirement. GICs can provide a reasonably secure investment, making them attractive in these cases. GICs may also be useful as a safe haven of extreme volatility in the stock or bond markets. GICs may not be the answer to all your investment needs, but they contribute to a diversified investment plan's overall stability.

IRAs. In addition to the tax advantages of retirement plan assets' tax-deferred compounding, you should note that withdrawals from most retirement plans other than required distributions are typically disadvantageous. Withdrawing from retirement plans before you absolutely have to will terminate the opportunity to receive tax-deferred compounding on the amount withdrawn; it may also result in the imposition of ordinary income tax as well as penalty tax on the amount withdrawn. For this reason, your most liquid investments should generally be held outside your retirement plans except to the extent of any retirement plan withdrawals you anticipate in the near term.

You should delay distributions from Roth IRAs for as long as possible since the income that builds up is tax free. Unlike with regular IRAs, you are not required to take any money out of your Roth IRA even after you reach age 70½.

7

PROTECTING YOUR FAMILY AND ASSETS THROUGH LIFE INSURANCE

Insurance takes the shape of an unusual form of investment: You pay for something you hope you never have occasion to use. Because of the irony inherent in this arrangement, some people hesitate to invest adequately in insurance coverage. This view, however, is a form of risky wishful thinking. Terrible events can befall even the most wonderful people. And even if you're single and have no obligations to anyone else, certain forms of insurance can save you from financial catastrophe. If you have a spouse and children, insurance is all the more crucial as a way for you to meet your obligations.

RISK MANAGEMENT AND INSURANCE CHOICES

Choices about insurance are, in fact, a subset of risk management, so let's start by considering how to identify and assess the risks you face. One way to undertake this process is to make a list of the fundamental risks:

- Death
- Disability
- Accidents or illness
- Property loss or damage
- Litigation for real or imagined negligence

> **Risk management:** *the discipline of determining how likely certain events will be, then deciding what steps will limit or transfer the consequences.*

Any of these events can cause you not just a severe personal crisis, but also a potential loss of income or liquidity affecting you, your family, or both. Risk management therefore serves as a way of limiting the negative consequences of such events.

Once you've identified at least the general kinds of risk you face, how can you limit them? You can limit some risks by decisions about how you live your life. Many of these decisions are obvious (although their obviousness doesn't seem to stop some people from ignoring them). Don't drive while drunk. Don't eat a high-fat diet. Don't take up hang gliding, ice climbing, or amateur bull fighting. In short, sensible choices about personal behavior can limit or even eliminate certain risks. However, given the inescapable nature of some risks—death being the most obvious—risk management sometimes functions more to reduce rather than to eliminate the effects of harmful events on your life. And one common way of reducing risk is to purchase insurance.

PLANNER

10 Big Mistakes in Insurance — #1
Knowingly underinsuring any major
risk that you could cover inexpensively

Insurance is essentially a means of transferring risk. Rather than risk all the consequences of physical disability, for instance, you pay a premium and transfer some of the risk to an insurance company. How much risk should you retain, and how much should you transfer? Those are essentially personal decisions, but here are some influencing factors:

- The degree of risk you're willing to tolerate
- The degree to which the risk can be transferred
- The likelihood of the risk affecting you
- The cost of transferring the risk

E
X
A
M
P
L
E
■ Sarah R. has an intense fear of earthquakes. Having lived through several recent quakes in California, she chose to leave that state rather than risk being there for the Big One. She's now living in Maine. She still worries about earthquakes, although she knows that quakes are unlikely in that part of the country. She's also aware that she could buy earthquake insurance to protect her against losses from property damage. Living in Maine, however, Sarah has only a slight risk of suffering death or property loss from an earthquake. Besides, coverage is expensive. Why bother? Under these conditions, it's reasonable for Sarah to retain the risk of earthquake damage rather than to transfer it. ■

E
X
A
M
P
L
E
■ Rick L. tends to dismiss the notion that he could suffer a disabling illness or accident. He's young, healthy, and careful; he can't image getting decked out from a medical problem. What Rick doesn't realize is that during youth, everyone has a much greater chance of being disabled than of dying. Disability insurance is quite expensive; still, the odds make it much more sensible to transfer this risk than to retain it. Despite Rick's confidence in his physical well-being, he should definitely obtain disability insurance. ■

In this chapter and the next, we explore the many ways in which insurance can transfer risk and, in so doing, provide financial and emotional well-being: financial well-being, because insurance can serve as a series of safety nets for you and your family; personal well-being, because the presence of these safety nets can significantly lower your level of worry.

Before considering the kinds of insurance you need, however, let's have a quick look at some kinds you probably don't need.

Inadvisable Insurance Products

Certain insurance products generally aren't worth the trouble or cost. Some of these products are useless; others respond to a legitimate purpose but cost too much; still others distract you from focusing on more urgent insurance needs. Here's a partial list of inadvisable insurance products:

Dread Disease Insurance. Dread disease policies generally duplicate coverage that's included under comprehensive health insurance programs—or ought to be.

Health Insurance on Pets. A pet's illness is unlikely to have severe financial consequences. Moreover, most health insurance policies for pets include many restrictions and are not automatically renewable.

Hospital Indemnity Insurance. Hospital indemnity policies pay you a predetermined amount for each day you are hospitalized. Although premiums are cheap—generally just a few hundred dollars per year—hospital indemnity insurance has minimal benefits: often as little as $100 per day. Their chief risk is distracting you from careful analysis of your comprehensive medical coverage, which should be increased if it's inadequate.

Credit Insurance. Many kinds of lenders—banks, credit card companies, auto dealers, retailers, and mortgage lenders—offer policies designed to pay your remaining balance in the event of your death or disability. Coverage of this sort may be a good idea; however, the coverage offered through these programs may not be as cost-effective as obtaining an individual term policy. (Note, however, that a term policy would cover your expenses only in the event of your death, not your disability).

As for the kinds of insurance you do need, life insurance is the first and certainly one of the most important.

LIFE INSURANCE

First of all, everything you do about life insurance will be meaningless if you don't accept your own mortality and your family's needs in the aftermath of your death. This may sound self-evident; however, a remarkable number of people speak of their own death in terms of *if*, not *when*.

So the starting point for a discussion of life insurance is literally to imagine that you're going to die tomorrow. Then sit down and figure out what you want to happen afterward. Obviously, the answer will depend on the specifics of your own particular circumstances—whether you're single or married, whether you have children or not, and so forth. Family structures have enormous impact on the discussion. For the moment, however, let's assume the "traditional" family of husband, wife, and 2.3 kids. What are the things you want taken care of following your death?

There are two main branches to the discussion and analysis: (1) needs for immediate and intermediate-term cash, and (2) long-term income continuation.

Needs for Immediate and Intermediate-Term Cash

First, your dependents will need cash for the first few weeks and months after you die. Typical expenses usually fall into two categories:

Needs for Immediate Cash

- Emergency fund
- Funeral costs
- Medical bills
- Other bills

Cash to Be Used for the Intermediate Term or Set Aside for the Longer Term

- Federal or state taxes
- Mortgage payoff (if advisable)
- Spouse's education or retraining costs
- Children's education costs (present or future)

When you consider this list, it's not hard to see why a significant amount of money may be needed in both the short and intermediate term.

Income Continuation

There are also the issues of how much income your family needs after you die, and how long that income should continue. This is the second main branch of the analysis.

The relatively easy part of analyzing income continuation is toting up the expenses you anticipate. Here are the typical categories of expenses for income continuation:

- Mortgage payments (if the mortgage hasn't been paid off)
- Rent
- Taxes (other than those withheld)
- Food
- Child care
- Utilities and fuel
- Insurance premiums
- Household maintenance
- Auto and other transportation expenses

- Loan payments
- Medical bills (other than those covered by insurance)
- Clothing expenses
- Savings and investments
- Charity
- Recreation and entertainment
- Miscellaneous

Estimating your expenditures based on this list should give you a rough sense of your projected expenses. (The job will be easier and the results more precise, of course, if you have already established a budget. See Chapter 1 to review this subject.) Let's say that your spouse will need $4,000 per month. Where is the money going to come from? How long will that monthly sum be necessary—for the rest of his or her life, perhaps, or until your children leave for college? Meanwhile, don't forget the consequences of inflation, which will render $4,000 considerably less valuable in the long run.

Common sources of income for supporting a family following the income provider's death are:

- The survivor's salary
- Interest and dividends
- Rents received
- Social Security benefits
- Veterans' benefits
- Existing life insurance
- Income from decedent's employee benefits

Consider two important aspects of this situation.

PLANNER *Be realistic about your spouse's likely income.* This is especially relevant in situations where the spouse hasn't worked outside the home in some years. Here are some crucial questions to ask:

- What is the current job market in her or his field now?
- What after-tax income is likely given current economic conditions?
- How emotionally stressful will she or he find returning to outside employment?
- What are the likely costs of preemployment education or training?
- What are the additional costs of returning to work (attire, child care, etc.)?

Once you calculate the total income from these sources, you should ask *what are the influences that can diminish their real value?* You may value your 401(k) plan at $100,000, for instance, yet you should also factor in a 28% tax bite to determine its actual worth. Still another consideration is the "blackout" period for Social Security benefits. (Payments to the surviving parent stop when the child reaches 16; payments to the child stop when the child reaches 18. Payments to your spouse resume when he or she reaches age 60.) During this time, your spouse won't receive any Social Security benefits. In short, you should subject your analysis to as stringent a set of reality checks as possible.

When you've assessed the complete sources of income, put the sources up against the needs. The difference (and the difference is almost always shortfall) is your *capital gap.* If you're like most people, looking at your capital gap for the first time will be a huge shock. The gap is much bigger than you probably expected. The reason? What you'll need to provide $4,000 a month at 4% inflation rate for a spouse who is, say, 35 years old—a spouse who may have a life expectancy of 80—is an enormous sum of money. And remember, you're calculating the money you need *after* having taken many thousands of dollars off the top to pay off the mort-gage, educate the kids, and pay some taxes.

> **Capital gap:** the difference between the amount of money you have (or will have) and the amount of money you need to provide for the objectives you've identified.

Many people question the validity of these figures when they first see them. However, blaming the analysis that reveals your capital gap is like blaming the x-rays that reveal a medical problem. Throwing out a set of alarming x-rays won't make you healthy.

Facing the Situation

How, then, should you deal with your capital gap?

The first step, as when facing other worrisome situations, is not to panic. Denial and alarmism will only complicate your task.

The second step is to reach an agreement with your spouse on *the present value of your assets* and on *your financial objectives for the future, including what level of financial support your family will need in the event of your death*. Among the issues you need to explore when considering the aftermath of your death are:

- Does your spouse intend to work outside the home?
- Is this realistic, given his or her background and/or the job market?
- Does a return to work suit his or her own preferences?
- Is this eventuality preferable to the alternative of buying additional insurance *now*?

How you answer these questions is a personal matter, of course, though a financial advisor can assist in the process. Once you've reached an agreement, however, you can lock into a number that indicates your insurance need. And that is your true starting point in making decisions about life insurance.

Q: I've heard that I can determine my life insurance needs simply by quadrupling or quintupling my annual income. Is this true?

A: Sometimes this method works. Unfortunately, it often results in overkill or underkill—sometimes gross underkill. Like most rules of thumb, this one isn't terribly accurate. It certainly isn't a method that takes individual needs and circumstances into account. A more rigorous, personalized analysis can spare your family much worry and heartache—not to mention expense.

As you deal with the issue of your capital gap, there are two main questions to ask:

- What are your insurance needs now?
- What will your insurance needs be 10, 15, or 20 years from today?

If you were to die tomorrow, your family's needs would resemble what we discussed earlier: paying off the mortgage, funding education, providing income for your spouse. If you were to die 15 to 20 years from now, however, you might imagine that your insurance needs would diminish considerably. "My kids will have been educated and my mortgage will be pretty much paid off," you say, "so my spouse will need a lot less income."

Rather, the *complexion* of their needs will have changed, although the *amount* of the capital gap may not have changed.

E ■ At 35, Arthur N. had one set of life insurance needs, most
X of which focused on making sure that his family would have
A sufficient income and educational funds if he were to die.
M Fifteen years later Arthur's needs have changed but haven't
P disappeared. He has paid off his mortgage and provided for
L his children's education, but he and his wife now have retire-
E ment on their minds. Arthur has also done sufficiently well

financially that he has the beginnings of an estate tax problem to address. He has significant amounts of money locked into retirement plans. If he were to die tomorrow, he'd want his wife to let that money sit and compound rather than having her take it out as ordinary income now, and he'd want the estate to be able to pay his estate taxes. In short, Arthur's need for insurance hasn't magically changed all that much *in quantity*, although the specific *purposes* for insurance coverage have changed remarkably. ■

There's another reason for making specific, detailed plans in addressing your capital gap. As you begin to plan for retirement, you should pay closer attention to the tax and investment characteristics of insurance. Some policies may prove beneficial to your long-range retirement and investment plans. The reason is that certain life insurance products actually provide specific tax advantages that aren't related to capital needs analysis alone. (We'll address these issues shortly in discussions of insurance products.)

10 Big Mistakes in Insurance — #2
Naming minor children as beneficiaries of a life insurance policy

Term vs. Cash Value Insurance

Your most fundamental decision about insurance is whether to buy *term* or *cash value* (also called *permanent*) products. Both of these categories of insurance can have a legitimate place in your financial and estate planning. We'll consider each of the specific kinds shortly. First, however, let's consider the general issues involved.

As with other aspects of financial planning, rules of thumb concerning life insurance are common. One of the most common is "Buy term and invest the rest." (That is, since a term policy will be cheaper than a cash value policy for the same face amount, you should buy the term policy, then invest the difference between the annual term and the cash value premiums.) Another rule of thumb is "Buy term insurance for 'term' needs and cash value insurance for 'permanent' needs." As with other kinds of folk wisdom, there's some validity to these bits of advice; at the same time, they tend to oversimplify the situation, often to a risky degree.

Term Insurance in a Nutshell. Term insurance is simply that—insurance that covers a specific term. You pay your premiums; the insurance company pays a benefit if you die. The relatively low expense of term insurance is its chief advantage over cash value products. Unlike cash value insurance, however, term products have no savings or investment features. There are several kinds of term insurance (discussed below).

Cash Value Insurance in a Nutshell. By contrast, cash value insurance is initially more expensive than term but offers a wide variety of savings, investment, and payment options. A common comparison used to describe term and cash value products is that term insurance is analogous to renting a house, while cash value resembles purchasing a house with a mortgage.

How can you know whether to purchase term or cash value insurance? We'll examine in detail the various advantages and disadvantages of both kinds in a moment. First, here are some other issues that can influence your decisions.

Discretionary income. As noted earlier, term policies are initially cheaper than an equivalent face amount of cash value insurance. If you can afford only term insurance, you have no sensible choice but to buy term. However, if you have enough discretionary income to purchase whatever type of insurance you want (or at least enough to buy some cash value insurance in addition to term), you should examine your particular needs and consider their duration.

Duration of needs. Depending on your age, the type of policy, and other factors, a cash value policy may require at least 15 years to develop enough after-tax cash surrender value to beat a buy-term-and-invest-the-rest approach. (This assumes a reasonable after-tax return on the difference between the two premiums.) For this reason, term insurance is probably appropriate for needs you expect to exist for about 15 years, and perhaps up to 20. (Typical needs to consider: paying off a mortgage, funding a child's education, and funding a spouse's financial requirements.) Needs likely to exist for more than 15 to 20 years should probably be covered by some form of cash value insurance.

Long-term economics. Locking into a cash value policy may look more expensive in the short run, but it is, after all, *permanent* insurance; once covered, you may have the ability to maintain a level premium for the life of the coverage. By contrast, term insurance premiums increase at regular intervals (determined by the specific policy) and may become prohibitively expensive past middle age.

Investment discipline. The rule of thumb urging you to "buy term and invest the rest" assumes that you have enough investment discipline to follow through and really invest the extra money, let alone invest it well. Some people do; some don't. Unfortunately, even the best intentions don't guarantee that "the rest" will end up invested well—or invested anywhere at all.

**10 Big Mistakes in Insurance — #3
Using term insurance for
permanent insurance needs**

Term Insurance in Detail

Most buyers of term insurance purchase one of two kinds:

- Annually renewable term
- Level premium term

Annually Renewable Term. With annually renewable term insurance, you pay the premium and your policy remains in force. The benefit stays level; your premium goes up every year. Many policies distinguish between the "current premium" and "maximum guaranteed premium," which the company will specify in the policy. Annually renewable term is the most common form of term insurance.

> **Current premium:** what the insurance company is now charging and expects to charge for the coverage.
> **Maximum guaranteed premium:** what the insurance company is contractually able to charge for the coverage, if they so choose.

 Are there computer programs for analyzing my insurance needs?

 Good programs are available. However, even the best programs currently in use may not address all the relevant issues or personalize the solutions sufficiently.

Level Premium Term. Level premium term insurance costs more per year initially than the annually renewable kind, but the premiums stay level for a period of five, 10, 15, or even 20 years. There is no issue of a "current premium" vs. a "maximum guaranteed premium" during that period in which you've locked into a rate that continues for the term specified. You'll take a physical exam after the guarantee period, after which (assuming you pass) you are covered for another period of equal duration at excellent rates. If you fail to pass the exam, however, continuing coverage is much more expensive.

Other Issues Regarding Term Insurance. Next we note a few other factors to contemplate as you sort through decisions about term insurance.

Convertibility. Many policies allow you to convert from term to cash value insurance without evidence of insurability. The chief advantage here is that a temporary policy becomes permanent—an option particularly useful to policyholders whose health may have deteriorated at some point while holding term insurance. Converting a term policy may be the cheapest, the easiest, and sometimes the only way for such people to obtain life insurance given their state of health at that time.

Features included in some term policies. Insurance companies routinely offer several other features that can affect any of the basic kinds of term policies. The most common of these are *declining, decreasing,* or *reducing coverage*, which diminish the death benefit over time; and the *disability waiver*, which provides for automatic payment of the premium if you become disabled.

Advantages of guaranteed-level term policies. The most popular term policies nowadays are those that guarantee a 10- or 15-year lock on a given premium. Many people like the certainty that the 15-year lock provides; in addition, the premiums on such policies are much cheaper after a few years than the normal renewable premiums would be. The risk here, however, is that you may not be able to continue at the attractive rates once the term ends. A crisis can occur if you end up 13 or 14 years into a 15-year policy at a time when your health has deteriorated. You may now not qualify for the next round of attractive rates. (Bear in mind, however, that you may be able to convert the policy and thus avoid losing your insurance.) A related issue: Insurance regulators are currently concerned that 15-year fixed premium policies will strain some insurance companies' surpluses and reserves. As a result, the regulating authorities may move to reduce the attractiveness of this product option.

Advantages of convertible, annually renewable policies. By contrast, the annually renewable term policy may be ideal for you *as long as it's convertible to a cash value policy*. The reason for this opinion is that on a present-value basis, the annual renewable term insurance *may* be cheaper for the term during which you need the coverage. The big uncertainty here is that, lacking a crystal ball or divine guidance, you can't realistically know how long you're going to need the coverage.

When to convert a term policy to cash value insurance. Most term policies are convertible, although some convert more cheaply than others. When should you convert? In addition to converting when your health changes for the worse, you should consider conversion at any time when you've decided that you may as well purchase cash value insurance. One reason for doing so is strictly financial. If you see that you have more than a 15- to 20-year need for insurance, the cash buildup and tax advantages from a cash value policy will work to your advantage by enabling you to keep your premium level.

Cash Value Insurance in Detail

There are three basic kinds of cash value policies:

- Whole life
- Universal life
- Variable life

One feature that whole life, universal, and variable life insurance policies all have in common is that their cash value grows on a tax-deferred basis, much as is true for an IRA.

Whole Life. This is the traditional cash value insurance product. Whole life insurance is just that: a product designed to cover you for your whole life, with the premiums to be paid for your *whole life*. Whole life insurance offers distinct advantages and disadvantages over term.

First, the advantages:

- Fixed premium for the life of the policy
- Automatic savings program for the policyholder
- Cash values build on a tax-deferred basis
- Option to borrow from the cash value
- Option to use your cash value or dividends to pay the policy's premiums
- Option to convert cash value to an annuity at your retirement

The disadvantages are:

- Higher initial premiums
- A long-term commitment that may reduce your flexibility by locking you into a stream of payments

---

 Q: What is "ordinary life" insurance?

 A: It's whole life insurance under another name.

Whole life insurance is available in a variety of formats. The most common are:

- *Participating*, for which the company pays dividends to the policyholder. More accurately, the company *may* pay dividends. The dividends are, in fact, not guaranteed—either in terms of their amount or in terms of there being any dividends at all.
- *Interest-sensitive*. These policies may look and work the same as the participating kind; the so-called returns above the guarantees are called excess credits.

- *Indeterminate premium.* These have lower premiums than other kinds of whole life, but the insurance company retains the right to increase premiums up to a guaranteed level. There are no dividends and no excess credits.

Premium structures for either participating or nonparticipating policies can make use of various approaches to premiums. The most common is the *level premium* concept. Another is the *modified premium*, in which the premium might be $5,000 per year for the first 15 years; then, at year 16, it might double. Or there might be a *graded premium*—one that would increase for a certain number of years. There are also policies that are paid up after 10 or 20 years, or when you reach age 65. At such points, the policy has contractually received all the money needed to provide you with your insurance coverage.

Universal Life.　During the late 1970s and early 1980s, partly as a result of the high interest rates at that time, the insurance companies began to develop a new kind of policy. This is universal life. The premise with universal life is essentially to "buy term and invest the rest," but inside a single account designed with open architecture—one in which you are able to see your actual cost of insurance, the rate of interest credited on your cash value, and the amount of expenses against your cash value. (Note that with whole life insurance the consumer can't determine any of these factors. Compared to universal life, whole life is essentially a "black box.")

Some additional features and benefits of universal life insurance are:

- Flexibility in determining the policy's face amount
- Flexibility in determining premium payments
- Annual reports indicating present and projected insurance, cash value, fees, and so forth

As this list suggests, the most persuasive feature of universal life insurance is flexibility. Universal life even allows you (within certain limits) to determine your own premium. For instance, you can ask your insurance agent to calculate (given a reasonable rate of interest and the current cost of insurance) a level annual premium that will keep your policy in force indefinitely. Or you can ask the agent to show you the premium that, assuming you pay for 10 years and then stop, will also keep the policy in force. In short, you can have many of the advantages of whole life but considerably more flexibility.

Are there disadvantages to universal life policies? Predictably, there are. The main issue is that the flexibility can work against you. When you buy a universal life policy, it enables you to have a lower initial premium than for a comparable whole life policy. The lower initial premium, however, is predicated on the company's keeping its cost of insurance and interest rates at the level projected. Yet if the company eventually reduces its interest crediting or increases its cost of insurance, and if you fund your universal policy with too low a premium, your payments won't be sufficient to carry the policy over the long term. These policies therefore call for your eternal vigilance.

Bear in mind as well that the decision to use the lower premium is also a decision to pay that premium much longer than you'd otherwise need to pay an equivalent whole life premium. With a whole life policy, you'll be able to put away your checkbook sooner or later.

Variable Life. The third general kind of cash value insurance, variable life, differs from regular whole life and universal life products chiefly in allowing you more leeway in your investment choices. Unlike whole and universal life policies (for which insurance companies manage the underlying investments), variable life policies allow you to invest in various combinations of stock, bond, and money market funds. You can't select any investment you want; you have to work within the separate accounts that the company makes available to you for your particular product. Some companies use only their own funds, while others have assembled six, seven, 10, or even more separate outside funds to choose from. This may allow you to take advantage of the equities' returns over those from fixed income investments.

Variable life can take the form of *variable whole life* or *variable universal life*. Some advisors regard variable universal as the best of all possible insurance worlds, for it provides all the flexibility of universal life while giving you investment flexibility as well. Many people find that flexibility attractive. It means essentially that within certain limits, you can put more or less premium money into the policy in a given payment period; and you have a much higher degree of input over where the investment share of your premium will go.

What about disadvantages? These are the typical drawbacks:

- Fees for variable life policies are somewhat higher than for other types of insurance because of their administrative complexity.
- The investment flexibility that variable life products offer may "provide you with enough rope to hang yourself" because:
  - You may inadvertently underfund the death benefit portion of your policy.
  - Your investment decisions may not pan out as you anticipate.

These products—whether variable whole life or variable universal—are significantly more complicated than the regular insurance products. You need to work a lot harder to come to grips with the variable products than with other kinds. If you aren't prepared to spend some time and energy monitoring your investments, you may be better off in a traditional product with steady growth and lower internal charges.

Whether you choose to purchase term insurance, cash value insurance, or a combination, here are some factors you should consider regarding any policy.

Nonforfeiture Options

You have certain legal rights when you purchase insurance. Nonforfeiture options assure you that you will have some value at a given moment in time. Any cash value product must offer the consumer or policy owner certain nonforfeiture options that you can take your cash value and apply it in certain ways.

Dividend Options

In a participating policy (one that pays dividends) you have several options for applying the dividends. The usual options are:

- You can take them in cash.
- You can ask the company to apply the dividends to reduce the premium.
- You can ask the company to reinvest the dividends within the policy to buy paid-up additional insurance.
- You can ask the company to use the additions to buy term insurance.
- Paid-up additions are small, single-premium policies purchased at net rates (i.e., without commission) that have their own cash value and death benefits. Paid-up additions in turn pay their own dividends.

Settlement Options

When you die, your beneficiaries can take the insurance benefits as a lump-sum payment. However, other options exist for receiving insurance benefits. The most common are:

- Taking them in installments
- Leaving them invested to compound at interest
- Taking them as an annuity

Disability Waiver

A disability waiver means that if you become disabled, the life insurance company will take over the premium payments and relieve you of the obligation to pay any further premiums while you are disabled. For some policies, the waiver is for the entire premium; other policies simply waive the cost of insurance to enable you to maintain the coverage.

Final Considerations on Term vs. Cash Value Policies

Every life insurance policy is, at bottom, a term policy. Every policy provides a death benefit in exchange for premiums, and every policy factors in the company's administrative expenses. Beyond that, your decision is whether you want to buy basic term insurance or instead to buy a product with features allowing you to pre-fund future premiums with cash value. The virtue of cash value policies, however, is that they are constructed to allow a level premium and even (under some circumstances) for you to cease paying premiums at all without loss of coverage. This is simply not possible with straight term insurance.

Here are some final considerations about term vs. cash value insurance.

The Tax Advantages of Cash Value

Another factor affects primarily people with high incomes. Let's say that you're an executive whose deferred compensation includes both qualified and nonqualified plans. All of that income will come to you at retirement. However, let's also suppose that you still have some insurance needs today for survivor income: Your kids aren't quite grown yet. You can fund cash value policies that cover your insurance needs but also provide a means for building tax-deferred sums you may be able to take out in various tax-free ways. This is a marvelous tax diversification strategy while you're covering your life insurance needs. Theoretically, you could buy term insurance to cover the remainder of your capital gap. But the cash value insurance can provide some retirement and investment planning flexibility that you wouldn't have later on without that insurance.

For Others, the Option for Greater Control Through Term

If, on the other hand, you feel confident that you really will "buy term and invest the rest," term may ultimately be your best product. The big issue here is control over your cash value. There are numerous shades of gray in this regard. If you invest in a whole life policy, you have no control over what the insurance company does with your money in its portfolio. A variable policy offers you considerably more flexibility for investment, plus the tax advantages of traditional insurance. Without question, however, "investing the rest" allows you the greatest leeway as to how you proceed. If you're convinced you have the knowledge and discipline to invest "the rest," go with term.

Life Insurance for Children

Finally, a difficult issue that can pertain equally to term or cash value insurance: the question of life insurance for children. Some people regard life insurance policies for children as inadvisable. They argue that your money would be far better spent on adding coverage for you and your spouse, whose death is statistically far more likely and would devastate your children's financial future. To some extent, there's a grain of truth in this attitude. However, the overall situation is more complex. There are, in fact, good reasons to take out life insurance on a child.

The Financial Impact of an Illness or Accident. If your child were to suffer a debilitating illness or accident and die, the resulting medical expenses could ruin you financially. Life insurance may serve to protect your family's well-being overall.

A Child's Policy as the "Ground Floor" for Later Coverage. Purchasing cash value insurance on a child may provide a relatively inexpensive "ground floor" for coverage that could last your son or daughter all the way through a long, healthy life. Alternatively, the coverage might end up even more important if your child ends up having difficulty obtaining life insurance later, given some sort of health problem.

The Hazards of Modern Life. The world is sufficiently hazardous that life insurance for a child isn't farfetched anyway.

Any or all of these considerations might justify purchasing life insurance for a child. At the same time, it's important to note that obtaining life insurance for children is, in fact, inappropriate *until the parents are adequately covered.*

Ways of Obtaining Life Insurance

Once you determine the amount and kind of life insurance you need, you should consider the options for obtaining a policy.

Purchase Through an Agent. This is the "traditional" way to obtain life insurance. The reasons for buying from an agent are that the agent:

- May represent a good company whose products are unavailable through other means of purchase
- May offer assistance in educating you about life insurance
- May have tools for determining your insurance needs

Part of your task in deciding whether or not to buy insurance from an agent, then, is to determine how much help you need, what sorts of companies you wish to purchase from, and who the agent represents. You want a qualified, credentialed insurance professional willing and able to "shop around" to find the product best suited to your needs. You want an agent who will assess the marketplace to a reasonable degree, attempting to match products to your specific situation. The insurance marketplace is filled with thousands of products; you can't expect an agent to check out every one. At the same time, given current technology for inputting specifications to define various policies' terms, you aren't asking too much of an agent to have him or her "run the numbers."

Direct Purchase. You can also buy insurance by telephoning any of several companies that are direct marketers. These are companies that sell various insurance products on a no-load basis with no sales commission. By purchasing from these companies, you are not dealing with an agent. You'll be dealing with the company's salaried representative, who will provide information about the products, including examples and quotes. Some of these representatives will be knowledgeable and helpful; however, others may not offer a high level of expertise.

Fee-for-Service Providers. A third route is to work with a fee-for-service (or fee-based) insurance provider. Such providers will charge you a fee for their time and effort to select a product that is either no load/no sales commission, or carries only a small commission. Fee-for-service providers earn their money through your fee. These, too, represent just a handful of companies. At the moment, there aren't many companies offering insurance by this means, but their number is growing.

Group Insurance. Finally, you can obtain insurance through your work. Many companies offer inexpensive term insurance policies. In addition, a fast-growing segment of the marketplace is group universal life insurance. If you're self-employed, you may be able to obtain insurance through professional associations—the bar association, accountants' associations, consultants' associations, and so forth.

Which of these means for obtaining insurance is best? This is a difficult question to answer. The most significant questions to ask about sources of coverage are:

- How much assistance do you need in selecting insurance products?
- What kind of value do you put on the professional relationship you have with the agent?
- To what degree does the counsel from a fee-for-service arrangement counterbalance the service provider's fee?
- Does the company you intend to buy from in fact provide its products only through agents?

Remember: *The bottom line is finding the right product.* With or without a commissioned agent, you want to buy the best policy you can afford from the best company you can find.

10 Big Mistakes in Insurance — #4 Calculating life insurance needs by rules of thumb rather than by assessing your actual circumstances

Rating Insurance Companies

Whatever source you choose for purchasing insurance, which companies warrant your trust? Generally speaking, consumers can obtain information about insurors from several independent firms that rate insurance companies' financial stability. These firms include A.M. Best, Duff & Phelps, Moody's Investors Service, Standard & Poor's (S&P) Corporation, and Weiss Research. Libraries, insurance agents, and the rating firms themselves are all convenient sources of the rating firms' data. You can obtain these ratings from your library, from your insurance agents, and sometimes from the rating firms themselves.

Once you have the data, however, a more difficult task begins: interpreting them. As so happens, the five firms noted above aren't consistent in how they present their ratings. Each has its own system, and the ratings don't necessarily correlate with one another. For example, A+ is A.M. Best's second-highest grade, but it's fifth from the top for S&P's and Duff & Phelps's, while Weiss Research grants an A+ rating to very few insurance companies at all. Trying to find a perfect correlation among the ratings for a particular company will be an exercise in frustration. On the other hand, if you take the various ratings and line them up, you will begin to see some patterns in how insurance companies stack up against one another. All the raters are examining the same features: the companies' financial strengths and weaknesses, momentum, and quality of management. However, even if you scrutinize insurance companies carefully, you run the risk of missing an important point.

Recent events within the insurance industry have created a "flight to quality" among insurance consumers. In and of itself, this emphasis on the carrier's quality isn't a bad thing; however, it's potentially problematic because *the strength of the company doesn't necessarily guarantee well-designed, competitively priced products.* It also doesn't necessarily follow that the companies with the highest ratings have provided the best values to their policyholders—or, for that matter, the products that best suit your needs. The rating firms rate companies, not products. You may have purchased a weak product from a strong company. Or you may have purchased a good product that's unnecessarily expensive.

Given this complex situation, what should you do?

First, your agent or financial counselor should establish the parameters for what you need in a policy. Perhaps what you need is, in fact, term insurance—or perhaps that's all you can afford. Perhaps you have the discretionary cash flow and long-term goals that make a cash value policy appropriate. Whether you choose term or cash value, the parameters you set indicate the kind of policy that the agent should obtain for you.

Second, your agent or counselor should size up the policy for its fundamental soundness. Checking the insurance company's ratings is a step in the right direction. However, the agent should also determine how the policy is constructed. What are its performance characteristics? What are its inherent risks? How does it compare with similar policies offered by other firms? By answering these questions, you can determine that the product from Company A is in fact built better and priced more competitively than the products from Companies B and C. In short, you should avoid the knee-jerk reaction to buy from the highest-rated company you can find. Set some minimum standards for your ratings, but spend as much time as possible on the competitiveness and credibility of the individual *product*.

8

PROTECTING YOUR FAMILY AND ASSETS THROUGH HEALTH, DISABILITY, PROPERTY/CASUALTY, AND AUTO INSURANCE

Life insurance is only the first of several kinds of insurance you need to protect yourself and your family from life's uncertainties. You need to protect your health as well—and your family's health. You need to protect yourself from the loss of income that a debilitating illness or accident might cause. Your home and car, too, must be insured. In this chapter, therefore, we delve into each of the kinds of insurance that provide protection against these risks.

HEALTH INSURANCE

Like life insurance, health insurance is a crucial component of risk management. Unlike life insurance, however, health insurance may be on the verge of major changes throughout the United States; reform proposals may alter how (and at what cost) many Americans receive health care coverage.

The fact that most Americans acquire health insurance through their workplace simplifies the situation to some extent; group coverage is typically cheaper, and often more complete, than what you can obtain as an individual. Yet even the work-related nature of health insurance in this country won't make all your decisions easy. Options abound, with more and more different programs to choose from. In addition to fee-for-service arrangements, you may have to consider choosing among health maintenance organizations (HMOs) or preferred provider organizations (PPOs). Losing your job throws the entire situation into a tailspin. Among the questions you'd have to ask at such a time are:

- What are your health insurance options while unemployed?
- How long can you retain your former coverage under the federal law called COBRA?
- What happens when that coverage expires?

And even if you remain happily employed until retirement, what happens after that? How will you close the many gaps in your Medicare coverage? It's no wonder that many Americans find the subject of health care profoundly worrisome.

10 Big Mistakes in Insurance — #5
Generally overestimating
coverage under Medicare

How Much Health Care Insurance Is Enough?

Unless you're independently wealthy, you simply must have health care coverage. Even a relatively "minor" hospitalization—a hernia operation, for instance, or a few days' medical observation following a car accident—can cost you thousands of dollars. A major illness or accident requiring multiple surgeries, expensive drugs, physical therapy, and a protracted hospital stay can easily leave you bankrupt. Responding to the question, "How much is enough?" the glib answer is clearly "As much as possible." The reality is that you probably don't have a whole lot of choice in the matter; health care plans come to you as precisely that—*plans*. You may have some latitude regarding which plan you choose or regarding how much of that particular plan you select, but it's hard to customize your own health insurance the way that you might customize your life insurance policies. Specific limitations may apply because of the nature of your family, your health, any preexisting conditions, and so forth. In addition, the appropriateness of coverage isn't simply a matter of the total coverage you can receive. Other crucial factors include deductibles, co-payments, and stop-loss provisions. Before we consider how these specific issues add up, however, let's look at the general forms that health insurance currently takes.

Kinds of Health Care Coverage

Most Americans pay for their health care coverage through one of the following methods:

- Fee-for-service policies
- Health maintenance organizations (HMOs)
- Preferred provider organizations (PPOs)

At the moment, fee-for-service arrangements predominate, but HMOs and PPOs are increasing in number and popularity. Future health care reforms may tip the balance further.

Fee-for-Service Policies. This form of coverage allows you the greatest leeway in selecting physicians and other health care providers. You receive treatment; the insurance company then pays some or all of your medical bills. The level of coverage depends on the specific plan you have joined. Here are the most common forms of coverage:

- *Basic:* includes hospitalization, inpatient nursing services, supplies, x-rays, lab tests, and medications; surgical procedures and anesthesia; and doctors' fees for both in- and out-patient consultations.

- *Supplemental Major Medical:* augments the basic plan with backup coverage that covers most health care costs up to a predetermined limit.
- *Comprehensive Major Medical:* covers most medical costs up to a lifetime maximum.

 Q: Are dental bills covered under my health care insurance?

 A: Probably not. However, some policies include dental care as a rider to the main policy. You may also be able to obtain individual dental coverage.

Even within each of these three forms of coverage, however, many differences exist from one policy to another. Some of the differences focus on what conditions or treatments will or won't be covered; just as significant are differences between how (and how much) the company will pay of your expenses. The three big issues in this regard are deductibles, co-payments, and stop-loss provisions.

Deductibles are the amount you pay out-of-pocket before the insurance company starts to pay its contribution to your bill. Typical deductibles range from $100 to $1,000. Deductibles can differ as to amounts, when they apply, to whom they apply, and so forth. Generally, the higher your deductible, the lower your insurance premiums.

Co-payments are the portion (expressed as a percentage) of your bill that you pay over and above the deductible; the insurance company pays the rest. A typical co-payment is 20%.

Stop-loss provisions are the cutoff point after which you pay nothing more. Typical stop-loss provisions are about $2,000 to $2,500 per year.

Maximum benefit amount is the aggregate amount that the insurer will pay under the policy.

Combined, your deductible, co-payment, and stop-loss provision determine how much you will pay of your medical expenses.

PLANNER Selecting your deductible is an important consideration. How high a deductible should you choose for your policy? This is a difficult question to answer—one influenced heavily by individual circumstances.

If you're young and healthy, you can afford to have the higher deductible; you're treating your health care policy essentially as a catastrophic plan. Your risks tend to lie at one end of the extreme or the other: You either have a few minor colds and other minor illnesses, or you get hit by a truck. On the other hand, if you're older, if you have a family member who's sick a lot, or if you have a lot of kids, the higher deductible will cause you significant out-of-pocket expenses over the course of a year. There's no simple, certain way to predict what will be the right deductible. What you choose is partly just a factor of how much risk you're willing to tolerate and (just as important) how high a premium you're able to afford.

PLANNER For all policies, you should carefully check the following factors:

- What expenses are covered by the policy? What expenses are *not* covered?
- What are the deductibles, co-payments, and stop-loss provisions?

- What conditions or treatments are covered by the deductible?
- What is the company's maximum for payments?
- Are there interior limits within the policy—conditions and services that aren't covered?
- Is the plan guaranteed renewable and noncancelable?

Health Maintenance Organizations. With HMOs, you join the organization, pay your monthly fee, and receive your medical care, all under the umbrella of a single provider. The advantages for you are lower payments, significantly reduced paperwork, and potentially "one-stop shopping" for your health care needs. The disadvantage is chiefly the greater limitations as to which physicians and other providers you can choose. People enrolled in HMOs report widely varied levels of satisfaction with the arrangement; it's difficult to generalize about whether HMOs are "better" than fee-for-service arrangements in this sense. Statistically, however, HMOs are becoming more and more common in this country.

Should you consider joining a health maintenance organization? As we noted earlier, there are significant advantages but also genuine disadvantages to these programs. You should consider a whole range of issues before you decide. Increasingly, you may not have a choice in the matter of whether or not to join an HMO, since many companies that pay most or all of the health insurance costs for their employees are switching to only HMO coverage. If you work for other companies, you may have to pay for more of your health insurance premium if you choose a fee-for-service plan over an HMO.

Current relationships with physicians. Membership in an HMO means that you'll be using the organization's own doctors. If you have close patient–physician relationships with any doctors who aren't affiliated with the HMO you may find the switch disruptive.

Level of medical needs. The more numerous and chronic your medical needs, the more likely an HMO will pay off economically. However, you should check carefully to make sure that the HMO covers the specific conditions for which you and your family need treatment.

Travel issues. Since most HMOs are located in urban or suburban areas, your location may affect the convenience of travel to the organization's clinic and hospital. You should also consider whether the HMO offers reimbursement for medical care you receive while traveling outside the area. (Most HMOs reimburse for emergency care elsewhere, but not all will pay for nonemergencies.)

Quality of care. To the degree possible, try to assess the HMO's quality of care. Some organizations offer open-house tours and get-acquainted sessions during which you can see the facilities and ask questions about the program.

Costs. In addition to membership fees, what are the HMO's out-of-pocket expenses? HMOs often charge lower co-payments than fee-for-service programs do, but you should ask in detail what they are. Even if lower than for fee-for-service, they will add up quickly during an extended illness.

Preferred Provider Organizations. PPOs offer a compromise between the traditional fee-for-service programs, in which you have almost complete freedom to choose medical providers, and HMOs, in which you are essentially locked into one group of providers for your health care needs. Under a PPO arrangement, a carrier (your employer or professional association) has arranged discounts or other financial incentives with a certain group of health care providers. Such arrangements stipulate that the carrier will encourage its employees or members to seek service among the health care providers in exchange for lower fees. The employees receive less expensive medical care; the medical providers benefit from lower administrative costs.

Theoretically, you can be a member of a PPO and still receive care from any physician you choose. In practice, however, the situation is more complicated. You may receive care from any physician—even those who aren't on the preferred provider list—but the PPO won't pay for those other physicians at the reduced rates. You save money only if you stay with the approved list. In this sense, membership in a PPO could complicate your choices if you felt a need, for instance, to receive care from a noncovered specialist.

 Q: Does my employer provide health care insurance?

 A: You'll have to check with your personnel or employee benefits department to determine the answer. Most large and midsized companies currently offer their employees some form of health care coverage.

OTHER HEALTH CARE INSURANCE ISSUES

In addition to group or individual health care insurance, you should explore your options for other kinds of coverage. These are:

- Medicare
- Medigap
- Long-term care
- COBRA

Medicare, Medigap, and long-term care are all issues that affect you chiefly after retirement. COBRA, however, is something that can enter the picture at any point in your adult life.

Medicare. Medicare is a federal health insurance program for people 65 and older, people of any age with permanent kidney failure, and certain disabled people under 65. Your parents can enroll in Medicare by contacting the Social Security Administration 3 months before their sixty-fifth birthdays. They are then eligible for benefits under both parts of the Medicare program: Part A, which helps pay for inpatient hospital care; and Part B, which helps pay for doctors' services, medical supplies, and other health care expenses. (Part A is available free; Part B is available for a monthly premium.)

Although many people have no problem dealing with Medicare, you should make sure that your parents understand the benefits they receive through the program as well as what they don't receive. There are significant gaps in Medicare coverage. For instance, even inpatient hospital coverage through Medicare has the following deductibles, coinsurance payments, and exclusions in 1998:

- A $764 deductible on the first admission to the hospital during each benefit period
- A $191 daily coinsurance payment for days 61 through 90
- A $382 coinsurance payment for each "lifetime reserve day" used
- A limitation on the number of lifetime reserve days available and used on coverage beyond 90 days
- No coverage for the first three units of whole blood or packed cells used each year in connection with covered services
- No coverage for a private hospital room (unless medically necessary) or for a private-duty nurse
- No coverage for personal convenience items (e.g., telephone or TV) in a hospital room
- No coverage for care that isn't medically necessary, or for nonemergency care in a hospital unless certified by Medicare
- No coverage for care received outside the United States and its territories, except under limited circumstances in Canada and Mexico

Although numerous, the items on this list are just the start in what Medicare doesn't provide. Other gaps exist in skilled nursing facility care, home health care, hospice care, and psychiatric care coverage. In short, your parents will be better off having Medicare than not having it, but their health care needs aren't adequately covered unless they have some other form of coverage to close the various gaps.

Medigap Insurance. The answer to this dilemma is private health insurance of the sort now colloquially called *Medigap*. This coverage takes the form of a policy that your parents (or you yourself) purchase to supplement their Medicare benefits. At present, there are 10 separate forms of Medigap insurance, each of which offers a different set of benefits. These forms are regulated by federal and state law, and they are uniform in attributes from one company to another. To determine specifically what sort of Medigap insurance your parents need, consult with your parents and their insurance agent to review the possibilities.

Long-Term Care. One issue that many people face is how to meet their elderly parents' needs if they require long-term care. (Long-term care is defined as unskilled nursing care in a nursing home or convalescent facility, or its equivalent in the recipient's own home.) This situation can be problematic because care of this sort is expensive, yet it isn't covered by Medicare. As a result, your parents may end up needing long-term care, yet be unable to afford it. This can leave you in a situation where you must either foot the bill or provide your parents with this sort of care yourself.

One other consideration, however: If your parents are likely to need long-term care but are unable to pay for it, you might consider funding this potential cost in advance. This is obviously an option that not all families can afford. In cases where it's a possibility, though, it can pay off well in the long run.

There are two main ways to accomplish this goal. One is purchasing long-term care insurance for your parent. The other is investing money that would pay for long-term care if it becomes necessary. Long-term care coverage isn't cheap, but it will pay for nursing home, convalescent facility, or in-home care when it's needed. Given the costs of such care, paying long-term care insurance premiums may involve a relatively modest investment. However, if your parents never need long-term care, the premium dollars invested in the policy are lost forever.

The other alternative—investing money to pay for long-term care out-of-pocket—has the advantage of offering you more flexibility. If your parent needs long-term care, you'll have some funds available for this purpose. You could use the funds to pay for institutional care if that's the family consensus; on the other hand, you could use the money instead to pay for modifying or adding onto your house so that Mom or Dad could move in with you. If the need never arises, then you can direct your investment to other goals. If the need does arise, it may cost you more than long-term care insurance premiums would have.

COBRA. The Congressional Omnibus Budget Reconciliation Act (COBRA) is a law that allows you to continue your group health insurance coverage if you lose or leave your job under a variety of circumstances. COBRA's advantage is obvious: interim health care coverage at times of life transition. To obtain benefits, you must fill out the required forms at your employer's benefits office. Once the period of COBRA coverage expires, you may have the option of converting your old policy to individual coverage through the same carrier. Coverage of this sort will probably be more expensive and with more limited benefits than what you had formerly, but the policy may still be cheaper than what you could obtain on your own.

PLANNER You are not entitled to coverage under COBRA if you lose your job for cause or because of misconduct; however, it applies under the following circumstances:

- If your hours are cut so that you no longer qualify for health insurance coverage under your company's current plan
- If you lose your job for reasons other than misconduct
- If you leave a company to become self-employed
- If you leave a company because you became disabled
- If you are covered under your spouse's group plan and your spouse dies or becomes eligible for Medicare, or if you get divorced
- If you are too old to retain coverage under your parents' group plan
- If your spouse and dependents have group coverage through your retirement plan but the company files for Chapter 11 bankruptcy
- If your new policy has a waiting period for coverage

Coverage under these conditions varies. The final condition on this list offers coverage only for the waiting period. Quitting your job allows 18 months of coverage. Disability allows 29 months. Widowhood, a spouse's eligibility for Medicare, divorce, a company's bankruptcy, or disqualification from group coverage because of your age all allow 36 months.

An important warning: Coordinating COBRA benefits at the time of retirement is potentially tricky. Suppose that you retire at age 65. At that point you will be eligible for Medicare. As regards your individual situation, you're home-free. Suppose, however, that your spouse is only 60 when you retire. Your spouse will receive health care coverage through COBRA until age 63. The problem is that your spouse will then have a gap of two years between the end of COBRA-mandated coverage and the onset of Medicare coverage—a gap that will occur at a time when many people experience a significantly increased need for medical services. If your spouse should suffer a major health problem during that gap in coverage, the financial consequences for both of you may be devastating.

10 Big Mistakes in Insurance — #6 Expecting Medicare to cover a sustained need for long-term care

DISABILITY INSURANCE

Many people who make thoughtful decisions about life insurance and health care coverage take little or no action to obtain disability insurance. The reasons are fairly simple. It's somehow easier to imagine getting sick or dying than being disabled. Or else the idea of disability is more alarming even than death. As a result, there's a temptation to put the whole thought out of mind.

The fact remains: If you're in your 30s or 40s, you have a much greater chance of being disabled than dying. (Or as someone put it, you're much more likely to be "laid up" than "laid out.") The risk of disability doesn't drop markedly until you reach your mid 50s. So the difficult question you should ask yourself is, "What would happen to my family finances if I had a heart attack or got hit by a car and couldn't work?" Once you recognize disability as a real possibility, you try to transfer the risk through insurance.

Q: How much disability coverage is enough?

A: Once again, as much as you can get. However, insurance providers are extremely cautious about how much coverage they allow; the amount you can get will be based in part on a straightforward percentage of your income. The rule of thumb is that you should try to have at least 60% of your income covered.

Group Disability Coverage

Your workplace may allow you access to the cheapest kind of disability coverage available, which is group or association disability. Coverage of this sort is basic, bread-and-butter disability insurance. It's cheap and fairly limited, but it has its advantages. Group coverage tends to be liberal in its definitions of disability for the first 2 years; many companies will define disability as your inability to perform *your own job*. After those two years, however, the companies become much more restrictive. Definitions of disability tend to be limited at that point to your inability to do *a* job. If you can be gainfully employed in some sense—even if the employment isn't your usual work—the insurance company probably won't consider you disabled at all.

An important tax consideration, however: If you pay your own disability premium and subsequently become disabled, the benefits you receive aren't taxable. However, if your employer pays your disability premiums, you will be taxed on the benefits.

Group disability policies have some other problems as well. They have limited features compared with individual policies. More significantly, they "cap out" at a specific amount per month that may not meet your expenses. Let's say you make $120,000 per year. Your group disability payments, however, are limited to $5,000 per month, or $60,000 per year. Assuming that you have fixed expenses of about $70,000 to $80,000 per year, how are you going to cover the gap between those expenses and your disability income? One possibility (depending on your employer) is to "wrap" an individual policy around your group coverage to close your capital gap. Another possibility is to find another carrier to sell you an individual policy that would provide the full disability income you need. In either case, the important thing is to compute your projected expenses realistically, then to find the best coverage you can afford.

Individual Disability Coverage

Once you've decided to obtain an individual policy and you've determined how much you want, you have many choices. You should check the following aspects of disability coverage, however, no matter what plan you're considering.

Definition of disability. Do you feel that you must be insured for your own specific occupation? Are you disabled *if you can't continue your usual work?* Or are you disabled *only if you can't work at all?* The definition of disability will affect what you pay for coverage, with a more specific definition costing more than a more general one.

Waiting period. How long must you wait before disability benefits begin? Typical waiting periods are 30, 60, 90, 120, and 180 days. The longer the wait, the lower your premiums. The price difference between a 30-day wait and a 180-day wait is significant; between 180 and 360 days, the difference is less dramatic. (The gap between the onset of disability and the onset of benefits will be more or less tolerable, depending on your company's sick-leave policies and short-term disability policies.)

 Is pregnancy covered under my disability insurance policy?

 Most policies do not cover normal pregnancies. However, they may cover disabilities that result from pregnancy.

Benefit period. This is the duration of the disability benefits. A longer benefit period means higher premiums.

Renewability and noncancelability. Your contract should be guaranteed renewable and noncancelable. A guaranteed-renewable, noncancelable policy means that the company can't cancel it if you continue paying the premiums. However, most companies will cancel the policy once you turn 65.

Cost-of-living escalator. Suppose that you buy $1,000 worth of benefits. Ten years from now, when you become disabled, you start getting your $1,000 monthly benefit, but every month the benefit goes up by 5%. This cost-of-living escalator covers for inflation.

Waiver of premium. This means that if you become disabled, you won't have to pay any premiums during the period of disability—a significant feature, considering the probable financial strains on you at the time.

PLANNER

10 Big Mistakes in Insurance — #7
Ignoring the need for disability insurance

Two final considerations. First, the most important aspect of disability insurance is simply that you *understand the need itself*. Few people can afford as much disability insurance as they ought to have. (The wealthier you are, the less probable it is that an insurance company will sell you enough to cover your expenses.) Being unable to close your capital gap completely, however, is no excuse for not trying to close it as much as possible.

Second, don't presume to rely on Social Security Disability Income (SSDI). SSDI does offer benefits in some instances, but only for severe, long-term disability. Most claims for SSDI are at least initially rejected. SSDI can become part of your disability income under certain circumstances, but it's not something you should count on.

PROPERTY/CASUALTY INSURANCE

We now move on to another category of insurance: policies that protect you and your family against economic losses from property damage and injury to other people. If you're like most people, you find the possibility of damage to your home or financial losses resulting from lawsuits almost as unpleasant as the notion of being disabled. And casualty and liability insurance is a subject you'd just as soon ignore altogether. Unfortunately, casualty/liability insurance resembles disability insurance in more ways than one. You are, in fact, at high risk of damage to your residence. Legal action against you is less likely, but almost anything is possible in our litigious society. And although you probably have some casualty/

liability insurance, you may be inadequately or improperly insured. You may feel confident that you have sufficient coverage, yet the aftermath of a fire, flood, or accident may reveal that your policy is full of gaps, caps, and exclusions.

Determining Your Level of Need

As with other kinds of insurance, determining your need for casualty and liability insurance starts with careful risk analysis. Some risks, such as fire, theft, and water damage, can affect all homeowners. Other risks—snow and ice damage, flooding, or earthquakes—are far more likely to threaten your property in some geographic areas than in others. The number of teenage drivers in your family, the kinds of cars you drive, the profession or trade you practice, and other factors all influence your risks for suffering an accident or being sued. So the first step in deciding on the level of casualty/liability insurance you need is realistically to take stock of the risks you face.

You can't determine need on a general basis, however, so your risk analysis should include a thorough inventory of your home and its contents. This step of the process is a good opportunity to begin accurate recordkeeping of what you own. At a minimum, you should photograph your household possessions; an increasing number of homeowners are using camcorders instead to obtain a more detailed record. Either method is fine, although camcorders probably allow you to gather a quicker, more detailed information about your possessions. Whether you photograph or videotape, however, you should also make a list of the possessions themselves, noting model and serial numbers, approximate purchase cost, and estimated replacement cost. (Your insurer may require an appraiser to estimate replacement costs for big-ticket items, including jewelry, silverware, art objects, and antiques.) Once you've finished making your list and visual record, keep both in a place *other* than your house.

The purpose of homeowners' insurance is to enable you to rebuild your home if it's damaged or destroyed and to replace

10 Big Mistakes in Insurance — #8 Carrying unrealistically low limits under your liability policies

belongings that end up stolen, destroyed, or damaged. For this reason, your goal in obtaining a policy is *to buy enough to replace most or all of your possessions that are at risk.* It's easy to underestimate your need. Many homeowners calculate their need for insurance on what they paid for their property or belongings years earlier; however, replacement or reconstruction usually costs far more now than before.

As always with insurance, the key issues for homeowners' insurance are:

- *The right policy.* Are the specific features of this insurance right for you?
- *Adequate breadth of coverage.* Are you covering what you need to cover?
- *Adequate limits.* Given your status in life, the value of your property, and the risks you're covering, is the amount of insurance truly adequate?
- *Competitive pricing.* Is this policy priced appropriately for what it offers?

The Two Aspects of Homeowners' Insurance

Homeowners' insurance includes two separate aspects: *property coverage* and *liability and medical payments.*

Property Coverage. Property coverage breaks down into three general categories.

Coverage A: House and grounds. Your coverage must be at least 80% of the replacement cost to get the full benefit of the policy;

otherwise, the benefits are limited to the actual cash value—which is replacement cost minus depreciation. What you want for Coverage A, however, is 100% guaranteed replacement coverage, 100% of replacement cost. That is, the insurer will replace the property *no matter what it costs to do so.* Older homes, especially, may cost vastly more to repair or replace than you would estimate. However, you may find that guaranteed replacement coverage for older homes is difficult to obtain.

Coverage B: Other structures. Amounting to 10% of Coverage A, this insures your unattached garage, tool shed, or other outbuildings on your property.

Coverage C: Contents. This coverage insures everything inside your home excepting whatever may be specifically excluded; typical exclusions are gold, silver, and jewelry, which require separate riders. Coverage is generally 50% of Coverage A; however, there are specific limitations on certain items, such as watches, jewelry, and gold coins. Companies pay actual cash value—replacement less depreciation. You can pay a higher premium and obtain replacement cost as well as coverage for specific items. Some people, for instance, insist on 70% coverage to insure the contents of their dwelling.

 Does my homeowners' insurance cover loss of or damage to jewelry I've loaned to my children?

 You are generally covered if you loan jewelry to your children on an occasional basis.

Coverage D: Loss of use. This coverage allows you living expenses during the time required to repair or rebuild your house. The amount is 20% of Coverage A.

Note: Using specific riders, you can obtain more insurance for Coverages B, C, and D.

$ SAVER

Although these terms are common, you should shop around to find an insurer who offers a complete and competitively priced policy. Some companies sell package deals that may offer favorable terms, including:

- Higher internal limits
- Fewer exclusions
- More specific kinds of coverage

In addition, you should determine whether your insurance company offers discounts for certain precautions you may have taken. Typical discounts apply for safety measures such as:

- Smoke detectors
- Fire extinguishers
- Deadbolts
- Alarm systems

A good insurance agent can help you choose among the available possibilities and obtain the greatest number of discounts. Talk to your insurance agent about what's available. There may be some flexibility in determining what's the most cost-effective policy with the most reasonable deductible. Specific homeowners' policies take the following forms.

HO1—the basic policy—covers the following risks:

- Fire or lightning
- Windstorm or hail
- Explosion
- Riot or civil disturbance
- Damage from an aircraft
- Damage from a vehicle
- Smoke damage

- Vandalism or malicious mischief
- Theft
- Breakage of glass that is part of a building
- Volcanic eruption

10 Big Mistakes in Insurance — #9 Carrying inadequate deductibles on property/casualty insurance

HO2—broad coverage—covers all risks specified under HO1, as well as:

- Burglary
- Falling objects
- Weight of ice, snow, or sleet
- Freezing of plumbing, heating, or air-conditioning system, of an automatic fire protective sprinkler system, or of a household appliance
- Accidental discharge or overflow of water or steam from a plumbing, heating, or air-conditioning system
- Sudden and accidental discharge from an artificially generated electric current
- Sudden and accidental tearing apart, cracking, burning, or bulging of a heating, air-conditioning, or protective sprinkler system or of an appliance for heating water

HO3—special homeowners' coverage—covers all perils except those explicitly excluded from the contract, usually:

- Flood
- Earthquake
- War
- Nuclear accident

HO5—provides even broader coverage than HO3. This policy extends the all-risk coverage to your contents, as well as to your home, unattached property, and loss of use.

HO4 and HO6—provide coverage for renters and condo owners, respectively. (*Note:* HO4 and HO6 coverage apply only to the contents of an apartment or condo, not to its structure—property that the renter or condo dweller doesn't own.)

HO8 coverage is equivalent to HO1, but for older homes.

Personal Liability. Within personal liability insurance there are two subcategories: Coverage E (Personal Liability) and Coverage F (Medical Payments to Others).

Coverage E covers certain risks whether you are at home or away from home. The typical coverage is $100,000 per occurrence for your liability for bodily injury or property damage; however, the recommended amount is at least $300,000.

Coverage F pays up to $1,000 per person for medical bills if someone is injured on your property. You might want to increase this coverage to $5,000.

Keeping Your Policy Current

Once you've selected the appropriate policy, you shouldn't neglect to keep it current. Changes that may require more extensive coverage include remodeling a kitchen or other rooms, building an addition, and acquiring valuable possessions (artwork, antiques, computers, etc.).

Filing a Claim

In the event of property damage, loss, or theft, the obvious first step is reporting to your insurance agent. However, you should also photograph any damage and obtain your records (photographs, videotapes, and lists of property) to provide the insurance adjuster. It goes without saying that you should notify the police if a theft has occurred.

Here are some questions to ask your agent during your initial conversation:

- Does my policy cover the damage or loss?
- Does my claim exceed my deductible?
- How long will processing my claim take?
- What is the procedure for getting estimates on repairs or replacement?

No matter how congenial this exchange may go, you should follow up the initial conversation with a letter detailing the damage or loss. Include evidence for your claim: photographs, model and serial numbers of appliances, and descriptions of items affected.

In cases of damage to residences, you should also take action to prevent further damage (i.e., weather damage to leaky roof). Save all receipts for repairs. If the property damage requires you to seek temporary lodging, save all receipts for hotel and restaurant expenses.

The sequence of events after filing usually goes more or less as follows:

- The insurance agent and adjuster receive your information.
- They either accept or reject your claim.
- If they accept it, they offer you a settlement.
- You can accept this settlement or reject it.
- If you reject it, you can ask your agent for an explanation of its terms.
- If this explanation is unacceptable, you can negotiate a settlement until you're satisfied.
- If you remain dissatisfied or if your claim is rejected, you can appeal the settlement through the following steps (each of which you should explore fully before proceeding to the next).
  - Send your documentation to the insurance company's chief claims officer and explain the dispute.
  - Call the National Insurance Consumer Helpline (800/942-4242) for advice and assistance on your claim.

- Complain to your state insurance department.
- Have an independent arbiter decide if the settlement is fair.
- As a last resort, hire a lawyer and sue the insurance company to collect a fair settlement.

AUTOMOBILE INSURANCE

Personal auto policies are designed to cover your legal liabilities, injury to you and your family, and property damage. The coverage is broken down into Coverage A, B, C, and D.

Q: What if I have more than one car to insure?

A: You can insure several cars under one policy. In fact, you may well receive discounted rates on the second and subsequent cars.

Coverage A: Liability coverage. Bodily injury, pain and suffering, medical bills, funerals, lost income, and property damage to the other car. Recommended limits: $250,000 per individual; $500,000 per accident. Or: $500,000 as a single limit, with no reference to per-person maximums.

Coverage B: Medical payment coverage. Bills to the doctor if you're hurt in the car; it protects you (the insured), your family, and others. The standard coverage is $1,000, but $10,000 is recommended.

Coverage C: Protection from uninsured or underinsured drivers. This coverage protects you if you're hit by a car whose driver is uninsured or underinsured, or if you're hit while a pedestrian. The recommended limits are $250,000–$500,000.

Q: Does my auto insurance cover me if I'm traveling overseas?

A: No, you must obtain insurance from the rental company.

Coverage D: Physical damage. This takes shape either as *collision* or *comprehensive*. Collision is coverage for getting hit and goes up to the actual cash value of the vehicle. Comprehensive is all risks other than collision—fire, theft, and so forth. Recommendation: Take the highest affordable deductible.

10 Big Mistakes in Insurance—#10 Carrying collision coverage on an inexpensive automobile

UMBRELLA POLICIES

Finally, let's have a quick look at a form of insurance coverage that can protect you from financial losses exceeding what your typical property/casualty policies provide: umbrella liability insurance.

Umbrella policies are essentially extended personal liability coverage. Imagine, for instance, that someone suffers an accident on your property. Your liability coverage stops at $500,000. But the accident victim sues you for negligence and demands $1 million in damages. Under these circumstances, an umbrella policy will protect you for whatever amount you've chosen. Typical face amounts range from $1 to $5 million. Policies of this sort include coverage of your home, automobiles, other vehicles (boats, snowmobiles, etc.), and other property. In most cases, they also cover you against suits for slander, defamation, libel, and plagiarism. (The exceptions apply to professional writers.)

Surprisingly, umbrella policies are fairly cheap. The main reason for their affordability is that their payout occurs only on an excess basis. Their nature limits the number of claims that insurance companies actually receive, since they are statistically far less frequent than other types of claims. Don't let the slim chances of having to file deter you from owning this kind of coverage: Not having an umbrella policy is one of the biggest insurance mistakes you can make.

> **Excess basis:** *claims that exceed what your other policies have already covered.*

This image of the umbrella is potentially useful in perceiving how all insurance coverage works. An umbrella protects you from misfortunes that might rain down on you and your family. A better image, however, might be that of the safety net: something that catches you if you slip and, precisely by catching you, prevents a mishap from being catastrophic. Obviously, any number of images serve the purpose. What matters is that you perceive the need for insurance, you analyze your insurance needs, and you select your specific policies carefully.

Insurance doesn't simply catch you when you fall; it also eases your anxieties about the risks inherent in being human, thus allowing you to focus on life itself rather than worrying about threats to your well-being.

9

PROVIDING FOR YOUR FAMILY THROUGH ESTATE PLANNING

Like insurance, estate planning is one of those subjects you'd probably prefer to avoid altogether. Benjamin Franklin said long ago that "Nothing is certain except death and taxes," and estate planning strikes many people as unpleasant in part because it requires thinking about *both* of these topics simultaneously. The fact remains: Estate planning is crucial as a means of providing for your family over the long term. Failing to plan for the legal and financial aftermath of your death won't spare your loved ones from the consequences; on the contrary, they'll simply have less control (and more bureaucratic hassle) than they would have otherwise. The possible results of failure to plan range from inconvenience to catastrophe.

In planning your estate, it's usually later than you think, but it's never *too* late. The big hurdle is simply getting started. The best way to begin the process is to follow six steps:

- *Step 1*: Calculate your estate's size.
- *Step 2*: Decide on your objectives.
- *Step 3*: Keep your plan flexible.
- *Step 4*: Provide for liquidity.

- *Step 5*: Aim to minimize taxes.
- *Step 6*: Schedule periodic reviews.

STEP 1 CALCULATE YOUR ESTATE

Calculating your estate's size is crucial for at least three reasons:

- You simply should have an overview of the assets you hold and what they're worth.
- Your estate—and therefore your potential tax liability— may turn out to be larger than you imagine. This is true for many people, including most who purchased a house or other real property before the 1980s boom.
- What you own and how much the assets are worth will determine many of your estate planning strategies.

If you've filled out the net worth (assets and liabilities) work-sheet in Chapter 1, you've already done what you need for this exercise. If not, you should use it now. The assets and liabilities worksheet (modified slightly to account for assets receivable at death) appears on page 203.

By subtracting your total liabilities from your total assets, you'll have an idea of your estate's taxable value. This will enable you to have a clearer picture of where you stand regarding your assets and liabilities; from there you can start to determine estate planning objectives. Two important considerations, however:

First, when indicating an asset's worth, *be sure to specify its current fair market value*. What you paid at the time of purchase doesn't count. Thus, the purchase price for your home in 1973 isn't the issue; rather, it's what you could sell the house for *now*. Similarly, you should calculate the value of stocks, bonds, and other investments as accurately as possible.

Second, *beware of hidden assets*. You may neglect to consider certain items that are, in fact, part of your estate. For instance, many people don't realize that the proceeds from an insurance policy

ASSETS AND LIABILITIES WORKSHEET

ASSETS*

Cash equivalents

Checking accounts	$_____
Savings accounts	_____
Money market accounts	_____
Money market fund accounts	_____
Certificates of deposit	_____
U.S. Treasury bills	_____
Death benefits of life insurance (with cash value of life insurance)	_____
Total	$_____

Investments

Stocks	_____
Bonds	_____
Mutual fund investments	_____
Partnership interests	_____
Other investments	_____
Total	$_____

Retirement funds

Pension (present lump-sum value)	_____
Joint and survivor annuities (present value)	_____
IRAs and Keogh accounts	_____
Employee savings plans [e.g., 401(k)]	_____
Total	$_____

Personal assets

Principal residence	$_____
Second residence	_____
Collectibles/art/ antiques	_____
Automobiles	_____
Home furnishings	_____
Furs and jewelry	_____
Other assets	_____
Total	$_____
Total assets	$_____

LIABILITIES

Charge account balances	_____
Personal loans	_____
Investment loans (margin, real estate, etc.)	_____
Home mortgages	_____
Home equity loans	_____
Alimony	_____
Child support	_____
Life insurance policy loans	_____

Projected income tax liability	_____
Estate settlement costs	_____
Final medical costs	_____
Funeral expenses	_____
Other liabilities	_____
Total liabilities	$(_____)
Assets minus liabilities	$_____

*Your estate includes one-half of the value of assets you hold with your spouse as joint tenants with right of survivorship. Other jointly held assets are included in proportion to the amount you contributed to the asset's purchase.

are included in the taxable estate—even though they aren't subject to the court-administered probate process.

Here are some other items you should be sure to factor in as you calculate your estate:

- Automobiles
- Other vehicles (boats, etc.)
- Collectibles and art objects
- Antiques, including furniture
- Jewelry
- Intellectual property (patents, copyrights, etc.)
- Assets owned overseas

Here again, the governing principle is fair market value.

10 Big Mistakes in Estate Planning—#1 Omitting foreign-owned assets from your estate plan

If you're a U.S. citizen or reside in the U.S. and own any asset overseas, the assets are still subject to U.S. estate tax. Depending on the type of asset, the laws of the other country and whether the U.S. has a treaty with that country, tax may be owed to that country with the U.S. allowing a credit.

STEP 2 DECIDE ON YOUR OBJECTIVES

Any personal estate plan must meet your objectives and the objectives of your family. If it fails in this fundamental way, the plan isn't worth the time you invest in creating it. Your first step in making an estate plan is therefore to determine what you want to accomplish. Keep in mind that your objectives will almost certainly change over time; however, later steps in the estate planning process will accommodate these changes.

The Range of Possible Objectives

Deciding on objectives in an estate plan involves far more than just answering the question, "Who gets what when I die?" That issue isn't a minor detail, but it's not the only thing you should decide. Your decisions should also address these issues in the following order of priority:

Your Own Personal Needs and Wishes. Although estate planning serves essentially to look out for others' needs, you have every right to honor your own preferences.

Your Spouse's Needs and Wishes. If you're married, one of your primary goals is probably to place your surviving spouse in a financial position that lets him or her maintain the same standard of living that the two of you enjoyed during your time together. You may well want to provide enough money for special needs, such as educating children and providing for medical expenses and emergencies.

Tax Considerations. These are important but secondary to other issues. If you neglect to achieve your personal goals, you can't consider your financial plan successful no matter how much money you save in taxes.

PLANNER In addition to meeting your own needs and your family's needs, you may wish to provide funds for your heirs to:

- Supplement your children's income for normal living costs
- Buy a home
- Enter into a business venture
- Fund other appropriate endeavors

Estates and the Younger Generation

You should consider three important aspects of how estate planning can affect the younger generation.

First, *a plan that leaves too much money to children or young adults can have negative rather than positive consequences.* The ready availability of money may diminish or end the incentive to work; in addition, children may lose the joy and sense of reward from individual accomplishment.

Second, *some parents question their children's ability to manage significant sums of money prudently.* They may worry that their inheritance will be dissipated without proper supervision. In light of these considerations, you must decide how much property to leave to your family, to charity, or to others.

Third, *you must decide how much control over property each of your heirs should have,* and on what dates or at what ages to confer such control.

Estates and Closely Held Businesses

If you have an interest in a closely held business, you should consider to whom and in what manner you will dispose of the interest. You may wish to retain your interest in the business within your family, or eventually sell out to the other owners. In either case, you must plan now to achieve your objectives.

Q: What's the urgency about estate planning?

A: If you don't address the often perplexing and even unpleasant dilemmas involved in deciding who gets what, *someone else will eventually make those decisions for you.* Do you really want state law or an outsider to determine what happens? If not, you should clarify your goals and write them down. You can always rewrite them—and you should, in fact, probably do so from time to time.

STEP 3   KEEP YOUR PLAN FLEXIBLE

There are several fundamental ways to establish control over and yet maintain the flexibility of your estate. The two most important ways are *wills* and *revocable trusts*.

The Will

Your will is the primary means of controlling the disposition of your assets after you die. While the operation of law determines the disposition of certain property (such as jointly held property), your will generally determines who inherits property that is held in your name without beneficiary designations. It's hard to overstate the importance of having a valid, up-to-date will. If you don't have a will, you should have one written soon. If you do have a will, you should review it on a regular basis with your advisor.

If you die without a will—that is, *intestate*—your assets will be distributed according to state law regardless of your wishes. For example, state laws typically divide an intestate husband's property among his widow and children, even though he might have preferred that his wife have use of the entire estate during her life. In addition, a will enables you to designate a guardian for your minor children in the event that you and your spouse die simultaneously. In the absence of a designated guardian, a governmental agency will be responsible for selecting the person to raise your children. The choice may very well be someone that you yourself would never have chosen.

 Where's the best place to keep a will?

 Many people instinctively place the original of their will in their safe deposit box. However, this can be a mistake in those states, such as New York, where the box is sealed upon the death of the renter. That's because the original must be filed with the Register of Wills following your death to formally name your executor and to begin the probate process. In states where the box is sealed at death, this process can be delayed and additional costs may be incurred in order to open the box before an executor is named. It may be best to leave the original with the attorney who drafted the will. You should also keep copies of the will in your safe deposit box and in a safe place in your home so that it's quickly available when needed.

The Revocable Trust

Having an attorney write a current will for you (and your spouse) is the best way to ensure implementation of your plan. However, revocable trusts may be used along with a will to control the disposition of certain assets. (For a discussion of revocable trusts, see Chapter 12.)

> **Revocable trust:** *a living trust that can be amended, modified, or canceled at any time.*

Other Means of Maintaining Flexibility

Revocable trusts and wills are exceptionally flexible tools that can help you meet your present objectives. Generally, you may execute a will and a revocable trust and still be able to revise your estate plan at any time. These arrangements allow you to retain complete control over any property that will pass under the provisions of your will or that is included in your revocable trust. The catch is that assets disposed of either by a will or by a revocable trust will be included in your gross estate for estate tax purposes. (See Chapter 10 for a detailed discussion of estate tax.)

In addition to maintaining flexibility by means of the documentary form you choose (i.e., a will, a revocable trust, etc.), you can attain flexibility by other means. Two of the most common are a *power of appointment* and *careful management of your own affairs during life.*

Power of Appointment. Including a *power of appointment* in a trust instrument preserves a degree of flexibility. It gives the possessor the power to direct distribution of the trust property to satisfy the changing needs of your beneficiaries. By this means, trust assets can be distributed when the holder of the power—someone you trust—believes that the beneficiaries need them most at the time the power is exercised.

Managing Your Affairs During Disability. Providing flexibility in managing your affairs during life is also important. An effective durable power of attorney for both you and your spouse can ensure that someone you trust will have the authority to manage your assets in case of disability. To be durable (i.e., effective even in the event of physical or mental disability), the power of attorney must be drafted in accordance with the law of the state in which you intend to use it. (See Chapter 13 for a discussion of durable powers of attorney.)

Situations That Reduce Flexibility

Finally, here are three situations that can reduce flexibility:

- Joint ownership of property
- Gifts
- Irrevocable trusts

Joint Ownership of Property

Jointly owned property (i.e., property you hold with someone as *joint tenants with right of survivorship* or as *tenants by the entirety*) passes under local law to the survivor upon the death of the first joint owner. Thus the first decedent's will (or trust instrument) will have no effect on the disposition of such assets. Also, joint ownership can sometimes create tax problems. It's therefore preferable in most estates of around $600,000 to $1,500,000 to maintain joint ownership with right of survivorship *only for your residence and a working bank account.* (Ownership as tenants in common allows you to state to whom your interest should pass.) Furthermore, many states require that both joint tenants must act to make desired changes in ownership. This restriction can sometimes curtail freedom to sell assets, make gifts, transfer property into trusts, corporations or partnerships, and make other desirable arrangements.

10 Big Mistakes in Estate Planning — #2
Holding all assets jointly

If you hold all assets jointly, these assets pass by law to the survivor when one holder dies, which can render ineffective otherwise carefully constructed estate plans. For example, joint accounts set up for convenience with only one child can upset an equal distribution pattern in your will.

Gifts

To make a gift that's effective for tax purposes, you must part with control of the property. Consequently, gift giving is a highly inflexible arrangement and doesn't allow for changing circumstances. However, a gift program can often produce large tax savings; you should therefore consider it when gifts are otherwise appropriate. (See Chapter 11 for a detailed description of gifts, gift taxes, and gift programs.)

Irrevocable Trusts

Under the proper conditions, *irrevocable trusts* are useful and can provide the tax savings afforded by gifts. Although they are somewhat inflexible, they provide a greater degree of continued control over the property than do outright gifts. You should limit their use to situations where you can retain enough assets to allow you the flexibility to cope with unexpected changes in your objectives. (See Chapter 12 for a detailed discussion of irrevocable trusts.)

STEP 4   PROVIDE FOR LIQUIDITY

Depending on the size of your estate, a large portion of it may be needed to pay estate and inheritance taxes. Your family may require cash for various administrative and other expenses associated with your death. Typical expenses immediately following death include:

- Funeral expenses
- Executor's fees

- Legal fees
- Accounting fees
- Appraisal fees
- Medical expenses incurred during a final illness

Your estate must generally pay all debts outstanding at the time of your death; the exceptions are those that provide for a specified term of payment, such as a mortgage on your home. Your family will also need income to cover readjustment and living expenses. All of these expenses underscore the need for liquidity.

> **Liquidity:** in this context, your estate's ability to meet cash requirements arising at the time of your death.

Sources of Liquidity

Sources of cash under these circumstances include:

- Social Security benefits payable to your survivors
- Separate income-producing property
- Cash in the bank
- Certificates of deposit
- Life insurance proceeds
- Marketable securities
- Payouts from an employee benefit plan

In Chapter 13 we discuss some specific liquidity issues.

Closely Held Business Interests

PLANNER If your estate includes closely held business interests, you may wish to consider a *buy-sell agreement* (either with your co-owner or with the business entity) to ensure that these interests can be converted into cash or notes receivable following your death. Such agreements serve several purposes: to create cash at the time of death, to shift control of the entity, to secure continuity of management, or to accomplish other business and personal objectives.

Nonliquid Assets and Their Consequences

Assets not readily convertible into cash may be of substantial value. Their value can increase estate taxes and other administration costs, however, since costs associated with insurance, appraisal, and management of such large holdings rise as the value rises. To complicate matters, these assets may not generate ready cash to meet expenses.

Nonliquid assets include:

- Real estate
- Closely held corporate stock
- Partnership interests
- Notes and mortgages
- Jewelry
- Art objects
- Antiques

If your estate contains a disproportionate amount of such nonliquid assets, you and your advisors can find several solutions to the problem.

E
X
A
M
P
L
E
◼ You may choose to write a definite plan for disposing of at least some of these assets during your lifetime, or you may make arrangements for an orderly sale at the time of your death. If you choose the latter, you'll have to work closely during your lifetime with the people you've selected to handle your estate after death. Even if you fail to prepare for sale, your executor may still be able to dispose of some of the nonliquid assets in an orderly way. ◼

Remember this point when deciding which assets to sell during life and which to keep: Appreciated assets will trigger a capital gains tax if sold during life, but will have their basis stepped up to fair market value if held at death. And when naming your executors in your will, consider selecting someone who has expertise in dealing with the types of assets that comprise your estate.

Special Tax Rules Can Help Relieve Liquidity Problems

If your estate meets certain technical requirements, special redemption provisions are available for closely held stock. Your estate may also be eligible for *paying estate taxes in installments* if an appropriate portion of it consists of an active trade or business. (For a discussion of these techniques, see Chapter 13.)

You may also qualify for (1) tax deferrals based on demonstrating "reasonable cause" or hardship, and (2) special valuations for certain real property.

STEP 5 AIM TO MINIMIZE TAXES

Assuming that your basic goal is to conserve as many of your assets as possible to benefit your heirs, minimizing taxes is a major consideration. Federal estate taxes and state inheritance taxes in some estates can erode your assets if you don't plan carefully. Next we look at some of the tools for trimming death taxes.

Marital Deduction. The *marital deduction* is a key tax-saver or tax-deferror designed for married couples. This subject is so important that we cover it in detail in Chapter 10.

Gifts and Charitable Contributions. Here are two more important ways to save taxes. However, these are sufficiently complex topics that we discuss them separately in Chapter 11.

Trusts. Here again, this is a topic of tax-saving programs that warrants a detailed discussion (see Chapter 12).

STEP 6	SCHEDULE PERIODIC REVIEWS

As noted earlier, your planning objectives are sure to change with new circumstances and needs. Certain life events can knock even the best-made estate plan out of kilter, and others can make fine-tuning necessary:

- Birth or adoption of children
- Death of a spouse or other heir
- Marriage
- Divorce
- Illness
- Educational needs
- Maturity of family members
- Employment change
- Receipt of a gift or inheritance
- Conversion of property to cash
- Changes in property values
- Changes in federal or state tax laws
- Changes in state property or probate laws
- Court decisions and government rulings

Keeping your plan flexible will enable you to make changes to meet altered circumstances; even so, obviously you must review the plan to determine where and when you need revisions. The only realistic way to do so is to establish a date when you and your spouse will review your plan. In fact, you should perform such a review at regular intervals—every September, for example.

If you take these six steps now, you'll be far ahead of the great majority of your fellow citizens—including a surprising number of those who have estates large enough to incur significant and unnecessary tax burdens simply because they've failed to plan.

ESTATE TAXES AND DEDUCTIONS

In Chapter 9 we outlined the six basic steps that should govern the estate planning process. Now let's consider the specific issues that influence the decisions you make. (We explore other subjects in Chapters 11 and 12 and conclude in Chapter 13.)

THE ABCS OF ESTATE TAX

Federal estate tax is a levy on the transfer of property at death. Your gross estate will include the fair market value of all property to the extent of your interest in it at the time of your death.

Assets Subject to Estate Tax

Here are the types of property included by law in your gross estate:

- Tangible personal property, real estate, and other assets
- Jointly owned property
- Life insurance
- Employee benefits
- Certain gifts
- Gift tax paid within 3 years of death

Tangible Personal Property, Real Estate, and Other Assets.
This category includes property you own that is transmitted at death according to provisions of a will or state intestacy laws. Such property is commonly referred to as the *probate estate*. Examples of this category include:

- Real estate
- Stocks, bonds
- Furniture
- Personal effects
- Jewelry
- Works of art
- Interests in a partnership
- Interests in a sole proprietorship
- Bank accounts
- Promissory notes or other evidence of indebtedness

 What's the difference between personal property and real property?

 Real property is land and the buildings on land. Personal property is everything else—cash, stocks and bonds, autos, household items, clothing, jewelry, and so forth. Personal property also includes intellectual property—patents, copyrights, and trademarks.

Jointly Owned Property. Only one-half of the value of property that a husband and wife own as *joint tenants with right of survivorship* (or *tenants by the entirety*) is included in the estate of the first spouse to die. The marital deduction prevents the property transfer from actually causing federal estate tax to be owed. Upon the survivor's death, however, the entire property will be subject to tax (assuming that it's still held at the time of death). See the second half of this chapter for more information on the marital deduction.

If the joint tenants aren't married, the entire value of the property is included in the gross estate of the first to die unless the estate can prove that the other joint owner actually furnished all or part of the payment for acquiring the property. If you and another joint owner acquired property by gift or inheritance, only your fractional share of the property is included. Similarly, if you hold property as a tenant in common with someone else, your estate will include your fractional interest of the property's value.

Life Insurance. Your gross estate will include life insurance proceeds that are receivable (1) by your estate or (2) by other beneficiaries if you possess any *incidents of ownership* in the policies at the time of your death.

 What do the incidents of ownership include?

 They are:

- The power to change the beneficiary of the policy
- The right to cancel the policy and receive the cash value
- The right to borrow against the policy
- The right to assign the policy

If someone else owns the policy on your life from its inception, the policy's proceeds aren't part of your estate. Also, if you transfer a policy to another party or to a trust and retain no incidents of ownership, the proceeds will generally be removed from your estate once you have survived for 3 years after the gift.

Employee Benefits. The value of payments from qualified pension plans and other retirement plans payable to surviving beneficiaries of an employee (or owner, in the case of a Keogh plan) is generally included in the decedent's gross estate.

Certain Gifts and Gift Tax Paid Within Three Years of Death. Gifts of property made during your lifetime generally aren't included in your gross estate, but they must be figured in the estate tax calculation if they exceed the $10,000 annual gift tax exclusion (see Chapter 11). As noted above, however, life insurance proceeds are includable if you gave away the policies or incidents of ownership within 3 years of your death. Also included is any gift tax you paid within 3 years of your death. Finally, lifetime gifts in which you retain some interest (e.g., life income interest) or control (e.g., voting rights in gifted stock) will be included in your gross estate.

Allowable Deductions

You can deduct expenses for:

- Funerals
- The estate's administration
- Debts
- Unpaid mortgages
- Other indebtedness on property included in the gross estate

Also allowed are such special deductions as the marital deduction and the charitable deduction. (See the second half of this chapter for details on these deductions.)

Funeral and Administration Expenses

Deductible funeral expenses include:

- Burial costs, such as expenditures for a tombstone, monument, or mausoleum
- Costs for a burial lot
- Costs for future care of a gravesite
- Other related costs

Deductible administration costs include:

- Executor's commissions
- Attorney's fees
- Accounting fees
- Appraisal fees
- Court costs
- Other related costs

Other Deductible Estate Expenses

To be deductible, debts must be enforceable personal obligations. Typical examples are your outstanding mortgage or personal bank loan, auto loan, credit card balances, utility bills, and so forth. The deductible amount includes any interest accrued on the debt at the time of your death. Transfers made under a marital property settlement incident to a divorce may be treated as estate expenses. Taxes are also deductible debts if they are accrued and unpaid at the time of your death. Deductible taxes include accrued property taxes, gift taxes unpaid at death, and income taxes. For example, if someone dies in February and his or her income tax return filed for the preceding year reports tax due of $2,000, that amount is a deductible estate expense.

Valuation of Estate Property

Property is included in an estate at its fair market value. Property that trades on an established market may be valued easily. For example, publicly traded stocks and bonds are valued based on the average of the high and low selling price on the date of death (or, if elected, the date 6 months after death). However, interests in closely held businesses or partnerships must generally be appraised to take the business's assets, earning capacity, and other factors into account. You're probably familiar with the process of getting a home appraised for purposes of obtaining a mortgage or home equity loan. It's especially important to have a certified appraiser with expertise in appraising the type of property that needs to be appraised. A CPA, attorney, or personal financial planner can assist in identifying an appropriate person to appraise business interests or other difficult-to-value property for estate or gift tax valuation purposes.

PLANNER Your gross estate is valued as of the *date of your death* or *6 months later*, whichever your personal representative elects. An election to value the estate 6 months after date of death will apply to all assets in the estate. Your executor can make the election only if doing so results in a decrease in estate tax liability. The amount remaining after subtracting any allowable deductions is your taxable estate; it's on this amount that the federal estate tax is computed.

Your executor should determine if using the alternate valuation date produces a tax advantage. He or she must then value all your assets on the date selected. The choice reflects any of several different strategies.

EXAMPLE ■ Suppose, for instance, that you died at the end of a bull market. Your assets might well be worth less 6 months after the date of your death; your executor thus has the opportunity to use the valuation on the 6-months-after-death date, which reduces the total size of your estate for tax purposes. However, the executor would have to value *all* your assets as of the alternate date. If your house and other tangible assets were appreciating while your stocks were depreciating, the big question would be how everything would balance out. ■

Tax Rates

The federal estate tax is progressive in nature and ranges from the lowest rate of 18% up to a rate of 55% for estates larger than $3 million. There's an additional 5% tax on taxable estates between $10 million and $20 million. The following table shows illustrative estate tax calculations.

ILLUSTRATIVE ESTATE TAX CALCULATIONS		
Taxable estate	Tax before credits	Marginal estate tax rate
$ 150,000	$ 38,800	32%
500,000	155,800	37%
1,000,000	345,800	41%
2,500,000	1,025,800	53%
3,000,000	1,290,800	55%
5,000,000	2,390,800	55%

Note: Each estate is allowed a unified credit.

Credits

In determining the net amount of federal estate tax due, your estate's personal representative can claim certain credits against your tentative tax:

- Unified estate and gift tax credit
- State death tax credit
- Foreign death tax credit
- Credit for tax on prior transfers

Unified Estate and Gift Tax Credit

The estate of each person dying in 1998 is entitled to a unified credit of $202,050—the amount of tax generated by a transfer of $625,000. The credit is called a *unified* credit because we have a unified system of gift and estate taxation, and because the credit applies against *both* gift and estate taxes. In other words, no estate or gift taxes will be assessed on the first $625,000 of your combined taxable gifts and transfers at death. You start owing tax once the aggregate amount of your taxable transfers during life and at death exceeds $625,000. At that point, the tax rates start with a 37% bracket and range as high as 55%. The unified credit equivalent amount is scheduled to increase through 2006 as follows:

1999	$650,000
2000 and 2001	$675,000
2002 and 2003	$700,000
2004	$850,000
2005	$950,000
2006 and thereafter	$1,000,000

E
X
A
M
P
L
E

■ Here's a very basic example. Suppose that your estate were $650,000. Your estate would owe no taxes on the first $625,000. For the remaining $25,000, you would owe tax at the 37% rate, or $9,250. ■

State Death Tax Credit

Your estate receives a credit for estate or inheritance taxes paid to any state or the District of Columbia. The tax must actually be paid on property included in the gross estate. The credit is limited to an amount computed under a graduated rate table based on the amount of the taxable estate reduced by $60,000. Most states only impose a tax on an estate in an amount designed to equal the credit allowable under the federal tax system. This type of state tax is called a "soak-up" (or "pick-up") tax because it *soaks up* the federal credit allowed. Some states do impose higher taxes, however. To the extent that the state death tax does exceed the credit allowed, the estate winds up bearing the extra expense.

Foreign Death Tax Credit

A credit is allowed against the federal estate tax for any death taxes actually paid to a foreign country, Puerto Rico, or the Virgin Islands on property that is also subject to the federal estate tax. The credit is limited to the U.S. tax attributable to the property taxed by the foreign country.

Credit for Tax on Prior Transfers

A credit is allowed against the federal estate tax for part or all of the estate tax paid on property transferred to you before your death or to your estate afterward from someone who died within 10 years before or 2 years after your death. An example might be if you died two years after receiving a bequest from a wealthy uncle. The credit prevents two successive taxes from being levied on the

> same property. Transferred property need not be identi-
> fied in your estate or even be in existence at the time of
> your death. It's sufficient that the transfer of property
> was subjected to federal estate tax in the other person's
> estate and that you died within the prescribed period.

State Tax Considerations

All states impose some kind of estate and/or inheritance tax. As
noted earlier, in many states the estate tax is simply a soak-up tax—
the amount of the federal credit for state death taxes. In these states
an estate that owes no federal estate tax because of the unified credit
will generally owe no state death taxes, either. But remember: Many
states impose an inheritance tax on the person that *receives* the
property from the decedent. This tax falls heaviest on bequests outside the immediate family. Therefore, in states that have estate or
inheritance taxes not tied to the federal credit or other federal rules
(such as the unlimited marital deduction), state death tax considerations may influence the form in which you should structure your
estate plan.

Illustrative Estate Tax Computations

Your personal representative will be responsible for computing
the estate tax for your estate and filing a tax return if the estate is
above $600,000. The tax will vary not only with the size of your
estate but also with the type of beneficiaries you've named, such
as a spouse or charity. Your personal representative will compute
your gross estate for estate tax purposes by totaling the fair market values of all your assets.

   In the tables that follow we show three examples for computing
the gross estate, the taxable estate, and the estate tax due for three
different-sized estates of married persons, each of whom was the
first of the two spouses to die.

COMPUTING THE GROSS ESTATE

	Tom	Harriet	Dick
Assets			
Cash	$ 3,000	$ 15,000	$ 60,000
Marketable securities	7,000	20,000	50,000
Business equity	0	450,000	525,000
Residence	200,000	260,000	185,000
Vacation residence	0	0	90,000
Personal property	95,000	25,000	40,000
Deferred compensation	105,000	25,000	75,000
Ordinary life insurance	10,000	80,000	570,000
Group-term insurance	50,000	50,000	75,000
Gross estate	$470,000	$925,000	$1,670,000

COMPUTING THE TAXABLE ESTATE

	Tom	Harriet	Dick
Gross estate	$470,000	$925,000	$1,670,000
Deductions			
Funeral expenses	3,000	4,000	6,000
Estate administration expenses	2,000	15,000	44,000
Debts	2,000	1,000	2,000
Mortgages	38,000	28,000	48,000
Marital deduction	425,000	250,000	550,000
Charitable deduction	0	2,000	20,000
Total deductions	$470,000	$300,000	$ 670,000
Taxable estate	$ 0	$625,000	$1,000,000

COMPUTING THE ESTATE TAX

	Tom	Harriet	Dick
Gross estate	$445,000	$925,000	$1,670,000
Deductions	445,000	300,000	670,000
Taxable Estate	0	625,000	1,000,000
Tentative tax	0	202,050	345,800
Unified credit	0	202,050	202,050
State tax credit	0	0	33,200
Estate tax	$ 0	$ 0	$ 110,550

E
X
A
M
P
L
E

■ At death, Tom had $3,000 in savings and checking accounts, 100 shares of marketable securities worth $70 each, and a residence worth $200,000. Tom's personal property consisted largely of a collection of rare coins valued at $80,000; the balance consisted of his car, clothing, and other personal effects. In addition, Tom had accumulated $105,000 in his employer's deferred bonus and 401(k) plans, and his estate was the beneficiary of one whole life policy and an employer-maintained group term policy.

Besides size, Harriet's and Dick's gross estates differ from Tom's in the following respects: Harriet was the sole proprietor of a consulting business valued at $450,000 at the time of her death, and Dick was a law firm partner whose interest was valued at $525,000 when he died. Dick also owned a beach house, which his father had willed to him outright.

Tom's will provided that his wife should receive his total estate after payment of debts, thereby reducing the taxable value of the estate to zero. Tom could do this because of the unlimited marital deduction (see the discussion of this topic that follows this example).

In Harriet's case, the size of her estate's marital deduction was the product of some planning. Harriet had designed her deduction to dovetail with the $625,000 unified credit equivalent, thus eliminating any estate tax liability. In other words, she left the first $625,000 of estate value to a trust that would generate tax and "use up" her unified credit; then she left the balance, or residue of her estate, to her husband.

Dick's estate used less than the full amount of the marital deduction needed to eliminate the estate tax; consequently, his estate paid some estate taxes at the lower marginal rates, even with the unified credit. Dick and his wife Elaine had decided that Elaine's anticipated financial needs would not require her outright ownership of all of Dick's estate, so Dick left the balance to his two sons, equally.

Remember that the unified credit equivalent is $625,000 in 1998; it increases until it reaches $1,000,000 by 2006. ■

These three examples show that computing federal estate tax is straightforward. The decedent's representative computes a tentative tax using the tax rate tables. Then the unified credit and any allowable credit for state death taxes paid are applied as direct, dollar-for-dollar offsets against the tentative tax specified in the federal estate tax tables for the taxable estate.

THE MARITAL DEDUCTION

Our second major topic for this chapter is the *marital deduction*— a feature of both the estate tax and the gift tax. If you're married, you are allowed an unlimited deduction for the value of property transferred to your spouse during life or at the time of your death. To put it bluntly: You can give or bequeath as much as you want to your spouse, and neither you nor your estate will pay gift or estate tax.

The estate tax marital deduction essentially permits you and your spouse to postpone paying estate tax until the second spouse dies. An important feature of the marital deduction is the flexibility to arrange the situation so that your spouse receives a lifetime income interest in the bequeathed property, while you determine who eventually receives that property.

Most married persons should take advantage of both the unified credit and the unlimited marital deduction to reduce the federal estate tax to zero in the estate of the first spouse to die. Harriet's case is an example of how to accomplish this goal. Her marital deduction bequest was calculated to be only $250,000 out of a gross estate of $925,000 (i.e., no more than the amount left after subtracting the unified credit equivalent of $625,000 and $50,000 of other deductions from the gross estate). As a result of using a "zero-tax" marital deduction, her estate paid no federal estate tax. You can tailor your marital bequest to your specifications. Tom used the full unlimited marital deduction, while Dick used less than the zero-tax amount in order to pay some estate taxes at the lower brackets.

The marital deduction is unavailable for property transferred by gift or at death to a donee or surviving spouse who isn't a U.S. citizen at the time of the transfer. Instead, the law provides that lifetime gifts to a non-U.S.-citizen spouse will be tax-free to the extent of $100,000 per year. Also, you can draft your will to place property in a special type of trust for the noncitizen spouse that will postpone the imposition of estate tax until either the property is distributed out of the trust or the surviving spouse dies. Called a Qualified Domestic Trust, it permits property to qualify for the marital deduction if certain requirements are met to prevent ultimate avoidance of the estate tax. Even if the decedent's spouse's will failed to provide for a Qualified Domestic Trust, the surviving spouse can create one and place the inherited assets in it to qualify for the marital deduction.

**10 Big Mistakes in Estate Planning—#3
Constructing an estate plan that
uses the marital deduction to reduce
estate taxes when a spouse who isn't
a U.S. citizen inherits property**

No estate tax marital deduction is available to recipient spouses who are not U.S. citizens.

The Estate Tax Marital Deduction

The estate tax marital deduction permits you to make unlimited transfers to a surviving spouse. The manner in which property passes to a surviving spouse is quite flexible. Property can pass through an outright bequest to the spouse or by operation of law (in the case of joint ownership of property with the right of survivorship). Alternatively, you can arrange for the use of trusts.

The marital deduction provisions ensure that the surviving spouse will actually receive the property to which the deduction relates (or at least the lifetime income from the property). It also ensures that unless subsequently disposed of in either a sale or a transfer subject to gift tax, this property will eventually be taxed in the surviving spouse's estate.

Life Insurance

Any life insurance proceeds included in your estate will qualify for the marital deduction if they are payable in a lump sum to your surviving spouse or to a trust that qualifies for the marital deduction. In addition, insurance proceeds will qualify under certain optional forms of settlement (e.g., an annuity) if either one of the following is true:

- The principal or any remaining unpaid installments are payable to your surviving spouse's estate upon death.
- Your surviving spouse is given a general power of appointment to designate the beneficiary of the principal remaining at death.

As we'll note later, using a life insurance trust will avoid tax on both estates.

Insurance policies offer a variety of options for paying the proceeds to the named beneficiaries. Having the proceeds paid in a lump sum is the most commonly used option. On the other hand, either you or the beneficiary may elect to have the proceeds paid in an annuity over the beneficiary's life.

If your spouse, as beneficiary, is in a financial position where he or she doesn't need the proceeds, some life insurance policies offer an "interest only" option, under which the survivor receives only interest on the principal for life. At death, the principal is paid to beneficiaries named by your spouse. This arrangement will qualify for the marital deduction, but the proceeds will be included in your spouse's estate. Also, insurance proceeds will qualify for the marital deduction, if they are paid to your spouse in a lump sum or in a life annuity with you (or your spouse) having the right to designate the beneficiary of any remaining guaranteed payments. As an additional benefit of using life insurance to provide for your beneficiaries, the proceeds are not subject to the probate process unless they are payable to your estate.

Estate Planning Considerations

Planning is crucial to secure the optimum estate tax marital deduction. Poor planning may result in transferring too much property to the surviving spouse—often referred to as "overfunding" the marital deduction. This would cause an unnecessarily large estate tax at the surviving spouse's death. Typically, you want to plan property transfers to maximize use of the marital deduction and both spouses' unified credits. Here are some alternatives to consider:

- Outright bequest to your spouse
- Jointly owned property
- Insurance arrangements
- Marital deduction trusts
- Marital deduction trusts with charitable remainders

Outright Bequest to Spouse

You can leave property outright to your spouse in your will. As a consequence, your spouse will have absolute ownership of the assets received and may do with them as he or she wishes. Outright bequests qualify for the marital deduction.

An outright transfer gives your spouse the greatest flexibility to react to changing circumstances after your death. On the other hand, outright transfers leave you with the least amount of continuing control over your property. When deciding whether you should leave property outright to your spouse, consider the following issues:

- Your spouse's experience in managing investments
- Your spouse's and other family members' anticipated financial needs
- Concerns you may have over how much of the property transferred to your spouse will eventually pass to your children or other selected heirs
- Whether your marital deduction will be overfunded

Jointly Owned Property

You and your spouse probably hold one or more bank accounts, your home, and perhaps other assets in joint names. In this case, the form of joint ownership will probably result in the property passing to the survivor by operation of law. Joint ownership is popular partly because these assets will avoid probate. However, joint holding of property where the property passes to your survivor removes some of your flexibility in planning for the transfer of those assets. The ownership of excessive amounts of jointly owned property between husband and wife can result in overfunding the marital deduction. This generally increases the amount of taxes that would otherwise be payable at the survivor's death without producing any additional savings in the first estate. You can't pay less than zero tax in the first estate!

Most advisors recommend very limited use of joint property ownership. For estates where combined family assets don't exceed the unified credit exemption amount, unlimited use of jointly owned property generally causes few problems. For larger estates, however, only your residence and a working bank account should usually be in joint names. If the sole joint tenants are husband and wife, only one-half of the property will be included in the estate of the first spouse to die. That one-half will qualify for the marital deduction, and its income tax basis will be stepped up to its fair market value at the date of the first spouse's death. The entire property will be subject to estate tax when the survivor dies (assuming the property is held at death).

Marital Deduction Trusts

For larger estates and estates containing closely held businesses, a marital deduction trust can often serve to provide you more control over assets while still qualifying for the marital deduction. This trust generally includes all property intended to qualify for the marital deduction, other than outright bequests and property interests passing by operation of law. One form of marital trust gives the survivor an income interest for life in the trust property and a general power of appointment exercisable during life or by will. This power enables the survivor to leave the trust property to anyone, including his or her own estate.

Q: Why should I use a marital deduction trust of this type?

A: The main reason is that you can appoint a trustee to control and manage property transferred during your surviving spouse's lifetime.

E
X
A
M
P
L
E

■ Let's say that you own a closely held business. Your spouse may not be sufficiently competent or experienced to manage the business effectively after your death. By setting up a general power of appointment marital deduction trust, you can vest voting control in another person (perhaps a family member) who is active in the company; at the same time you ensure that your spouse receives the income from the business during his or her lifetime and retains control over who will ultimately inherit the company. Giving your spouse control over ultimate disposition may be desirable in some cases, as when you want your spouse to distribute the property based on the children's circumstances at his or her death. ■

PLANNER Additional flexibility is available by using a *qualified terminal interest property (QTIP) trust* as the marital trust. A QTIP trust is an estate tax mechanism that allows you to provide a life income interest for your spouse while determining in *your* will who will take the property after your spouse's death. You can, if you wish, also give your spouse the power to appoint any remaining trust property among a limited class of persons (probably your children) in his or her will. The lifetime income requirement in any marital deduction trust is strict. It can't terminate after a given number of years or upon your spouse's remarriage.

A QTIP transfer qualifies for the marital deduction only to the extent that your executor elects to claim it. This actually provides added flexibility to the estate because it allows the executor to decide if there may be some tax advantage to be gained from paying tax in the first estate. Of course, the surviving spouse's taxable estate will include the portion of the trust property for which the marital deduction was elected.

The QTIP trust can be particularly appropriate when stock of a family business is involved and a family member other than the surviving spouse is active in the company. A QTIP trust is also a convenient way to assure your spouse adequate income during his or her life while ensuring that your assets ultimately go where you want them to go. Thus, if you have children from a previous marriage, or if your spouse remarries after your death, the children named in your will could be assured that they will be the eventual beneficiaries of your estate. This can provide a great sense of comfort: No matter what happens to your family structure following your death, your money will go to your children.

PLANNER A *bypass trust*—also called a *credit shelter* or *nonmarital trust*—is typically utilized in conjunction with a marital deduction trust. The bypass trust receives just enough assets to absorb the unified credit remaining at the decedent's death—$625,000 in 1998. Although the survivor will generally have an income interest in this trust and can receive trust principal if needed, he or she will have no power over the final disposition of the assets of the trust. It's called a bypass trust because the property, along with any appreciation and income accumulation, will bypass taxation in the surviving spouse's estate.

Marital Deduction Trust with Charitable Remainder

In another variation of the marital deduction trust, you can specify a qualified charitable organization to receive the property eventually. The trust would be established following the first spouse's death and would qualify for the marital deduction, since the survivor would be entitled to all the trust's income for life. Following the survivor's death, the property would be included in his or her estate but would not be subject to any federal estate tax, since it would pass to a qualified charity. This may be an ideal way of providing for your spouse and a favorite charity.

 Whom should I choose as my trustee?

 In some families, friction results from disagreements over whether the surviving spouse or someone else—perhaps a grown son or daughter—will administer the trust. You may choose to have your surviving spouse receive benefits from a trust that is intended to allow her or him to live comfortably, yet not necessarily serve as trustee. In a harmonious family, this won't present any problems; the surviving spouse will continue living as before, and the children will readily allow her or him any needed use of the money. In other cases, the situation won't be quite so harmonious, and the spouse or an independent advisor may need to serve alone or as co-trustees. In some cases, a bank or institutional trustee may be advisable if the assets in the trust need professional management. The upshot, then, is to choose carefully as you select both the trustee and the terms of the trust.

Optimum Use of the Marital Deduction

Marital deduction benefits are available during your lifetime or upon your death, and they can be tailored to meet your precise needs. However, planning is essential to obtain maximum benefits. Here's an example. The unlimited marital deduction can reduce your federal estate tax to zero; yet if you die without a will a state intestacy statute may provide that part of your estate will go to your children and not to your spouse. That portion of your estate will not qualify for the marital deduction.

As a result, your estate may pay estate taxes that could have been deferred through proper planning. However, if your spouse is well provided for in his or her own right, a marital bequest may burden his or her estate with significantly more tax than your estate would be saving. This can be especially true if the survivor's estate tax bracket is significantly increased above the bracket that would have applied in the first estate.

A reminder: Using the marital deduction doesn't permanently wipe out estate tax due on the assets owned by the first spouse to die. Instead, it merely *postpones* the payment of the tax until the surviving spouse's death. Be sure that both you and your spouse fully utilize your own unified credit equivalent before using the marital deduction. That is, you should leave property worth up to the unified credit equivalent to those beneficiaries you intend to receive the property after your spouse's death. By using a bypass trust, your spouse can have complete access to the income and principal if it's needed to live on. No estate tax will be due on any assets left in a bypass trust at your death or at your spouse's death, since the property will not be included in his or her estate.

10 Big Mistakes in Estate Planning — #4
Overusing the marital tax deduction

Although the IRS lets you and your spouse leave each other property free from estate tax, you may end up increasing your family's estate tax bill if you leave everything to your spouse. You end up forfeiting all or part of one of the unified credit equivalents available to each of you.

GIFT TAX FUNDAMENTALS AND GENERATION-SKIPPING TRANSFER TAX

The federal government imposes a substantial tax on gifts of money or property above certain levels. The reason? Without such a tax someone with a sizable estate could give away a large portion of their property before death and escape death taxes altogether. If you have a sizable estate, this probably sounds fine to you, but the government thinks otherwise. For this reason, the gift tax acts more or less as a backstop to the estate tax. And yet, few people actually pay a gift tax during their lifetime. A gift program can substantially reduce overall transfer taxes; however, it requires good planning and a commitment to proceed with the gifts before it's too late.

This chapter explores the following topics:

- The advantages of making gifts
- The generation-skipping transfer tax
- The excess accumulations tax

THE ADVANTAGES OF MAKING GIFTS

You may have many reasons for making gifts. Personal motives for gift giving may reflect your desire to:

- Assist someone in immediate financial need
- Provide financial or psychological security for the recipient
- Give the recipient experience in handling money
- See the recipient enjoy the property

 Are gifts of jewelry, art, and so on, subject to the same gift tax rules as gifts of money, stock, and so forth?

 Yes. The determining factor for gifts such as jewelry and art, as for other kinds of property, is fair market value.

In addition to satisfying your personal aims, gifts can bring certain tax advantages. The standard arrangements are:

- Annual exclusion gifts
- Marital deduction gifts
- No-gift-tax gift program
- Paying gift tax to reduce overall taxes
- Gifts to minors

Gift Tax Annual Exclusion

Probably the easiest way to reduce the size of your taxable estate is to make regular use of the gift tax annual exclusion. You may give up to $10,000 each year to as many persons as you want without incurring any gift tax. If your spouse joins in making the gift (by consenting on a gift tax return), you may (as a couple) give $20,000 to each person annually without any gift tax liability.

10 Big Mistakes in Estate Planning—#5
Failing to maximize usage of the annual $10,000 gift tax exclusion

This annual gift tax exclusion applies only to gifts of present interests. A present interest is the right to use, possess, or enjoy the gift property now or soon. Examples of a gift of a present interest include gifts of money, holiday presents, an income interest in a trust, and so forth. Gifts of future interests do not qualify for the exclusion. Gifts of future interests include reversions, remainder interests, and other interests that won't give the recipient the right to possess or enjoy the property until a future date or time. A gift of a future interest occurs when the beneficiary isn't entitled to immediate enjoyment of the gift property or its income. However, gifts in trust to minors are subject to special rules that may allow an otherwise future interest to qualify for the $10,000 exclusion. (See later sections of this chapter for a discussion of gifts to minors.)

In addition to the $10,000 exclusion, there is an *unlimited gift tax exclusion* available to pay someone's medical or educational expenses. The beneficiary doesn't have to be your dependent or even related to you, although payment of a grandchild's expenses is perhaps the most common use of the exclusion. You must make the payment *directly* to the institution providing the service—the beneficiary himself or herself must not receive the payment. Medical expenses can include health insurance premiums. Educational expenses are restricted to tuition; room and board, books, and other fees do not qualify for the unlimited exclusion, although they do, of course, qualify for the annual $10,000 exclusion. Given the high cost of education today, gifts of this sort can become a significant benefit for your family members or others you choose to be recipients.

PLANNER Make annual exclusion gifts at the beginning of the year—not as a Christmas or Hanukkah present. You'll remove an additional year's income and appreciation on the gifted property, which compounds over time.

Use of the gift tax exclusion in a single year may not affect your estate tax situation significantly, but you can reduce your taxable estate substantially through a planned annual program of $10,000 (or $20,000 if you're married) gifts. All gifts within the exclusion limits are protected from federal estate taxes and most types are protected from generation-skipping transfer taxes (see the discussion below).

In addition to reducing the size of your estate, another major tax advantage of making a gift is the removal of future appreciation in the property's value from your estate. Suppose that you give stocks worth $50,000 to your children now. If you die in 10 years and the stock is worth $130,000, your estate will escape tax on the $80,000 of appreciation.

10 Big Mistakes in Estate Planning—#6
Making gifts to someone who uses the money to pay for medical or educational expenses

Instead, you should pay for that person's medical or educational expenses directly, thus allowing you to exceed the $10,000 annual limit on tax-free gifts.

PLANNER You can also realize immediate income tax savings when you make gifts of income-producing property to a recipient in a lower-income tax bracket. However, you gain this tax benefit at the expense of forfeiting your future enjoyment and control over the gifted property. And such income-shifting opportunities have been sharply curtailed for gifts to children under age 14. That's due to the kiddie tax, which taxes unearned income over $1,400 (adjusted for inflation) of children under 14 at the higher of their parents' or their own tax rate.

There's an unlimited gift tax charitable deduction available for transfers to most charitable organizations. The effect of this deduction is to make such charitable donations nontaxable to the donor; it may also produce an income tax deduction.

Gift Tax Marital Deduction

The gift tax marital deduction allows you to transfer unlimited amounts of property during your lifetime to your spouse without gift tax. Property can be transferred outright or in trust. If structured properly, a gift of a lifetime income interest in property to your spouse can also qualify for the marital deduction.

The gift tax marital deduction can be a useful tool for minimizing taxes of a couple with combined assets over $625,000. Because each spouse can transfer $625,000 tax-free, a couple should be able to transfer up to $1,250,000 tax-free in 1998. But to obtain this benefit if your spouse has an estate of less than $625,000, you may need to make gifts to your spouse so that he or she will have an estate at least equal to the $625,000 credit equivalent amount. Using the gift tax marital deduction will facilitate such transfers.

Three caveats: First, as mentioned earlier, *the marital deduction isn't allowed for gifts to a spouse who is not a U.S. citizen.* Instead, the $10,000 annual exclusion available for present interest gifts is boosted to $100,000 if the recipient is a noncitizen spouse.

Second, *several states also impose a gift tax.* The amount of the gift tax marital deduction for state purposes may differ from the federal amount. It's crucial to get professional advice before making any significant gifts.

Third, *the credit equivalent amount increases in 1999 to $650,000 and then periodically afterwards until it reaches $1,000,000 in 2006.* As the credit equivalent increases you should make additional gifts of the amount of the increase.

A No-Gift-Tax Gift Program

E
X
A
M
P
L
E

■ Here's an example illustrating a substantial gift program that incurs no net gift tax. (Note, however, that part of the unified credit is being used.)

During the course of one year, James made outright gifts of $100,000 to his wife, Helen; $40,000 to each of his three children; and $30,000 to the United Way—for a total of $250,000. The table below illustrates computing the gift tax and shows why James owed no tax on these gifts.

COMPUTING GIFT TAX

	Wife	Three children	Charity	Total
Gifts by husband	$100,000	$120,000	$30,000	$250,000
Less:				
Annual exclusion, husband	10,000	30,000	10,000	50,000
Annual exclusion, wife	0	30,000	10,000	40,000
Marital deduction	90,000	0	0	90,000
Charitable deduction	0	0	10,000	10,000
Total deductions and exclusions	100,000	60,000	30,000	190,000
Taxable gifts	$ 0	$ 60,000	$ 0	$ 60,000

	Husband	Wife	Total
Tentative gift tax	$ 6,500	$ 6,500	$ 13,000
Unified gift and estate tax credit	6,500	6,500	13,000
Gift tax payable	$ 0	$ 0	$ 0

The Gift to Helen

James incurred no gift tax on Helen's gift because of the $10,000 annual exclusion and the unlimited marital deduction.

The Gifts to James's Three Children

James and Helen were entitled to a total of $60,000 in annual exclusions ($20,000 for each child) because they elected to consider one-half of those gifts as made by Helen. Nevertheless, a net taxable gift of $60,000 remains. By applying a portion of the unified credit as a dollar-for-dollar offset, James and Helen can entirely eliminate paying gift tax.

The Gift to the United Way

For gift tax purposes, James and Helen reduced the $30,000 by their combined $20,000 of exclusions. The remaining $10,000 qualified as a charitable deduction *for gift tax purposes.* In addition, the entire $30,000 charitable gift was deductible by James *for income tax purposes.* ■

Paying Gift Tax to Reduce Overall Taxes

Most of us have a natural aversion to paying taxes, and gift taxes are no exception. However, if you have a sizable estate—one considerably in excess of what you need to live on—you might do well to consider how paying gift taxes *now* can save on estate taxes *later.* The end result is that more of your assets bypass the IRS and actually reach your heirs.

There's a fundamental difference in how estate and gift taxes are calculated that explains why paying gift tax can save you overall transfer taxes. When you make a gift, the tax is computed only on the amount *actually received* by the donee. The gift tax is paid *in addition to* the gift and isn't part of the tax base, which is why the gift tax is called "tax-exclusive."

The estate tax, on the other hand, is computed on the *entire* value of property included in your gross estate—including the amount that will have to go toward paying the estate tax. The estate tax, therefore, is a "tax-inclusive" tax. Your heirs get only what's left after the tax is paid.

E X A M P L E ■ Here's how paying gift tax can put more money in your heirs' hands. We'll compare the situations of two women, Sarah and Marti. Each has survived her spouse. Each now has $2.5 million of liquid assets. Sarah holds on to the full $2.5 million until death, while Marti makes a gift of $1 million to her children (in addition to annual exclusion gifts). Assuming that neither had previously made taxable gifts and that Marti lives for 3 years after the gift, in the table below we show how their taxes would compare if they die in 1998.

COMPARISON OF GIFT TAXES FOR SARAH AND MARTI			
Sarah: No Gift		**Marti: Gift**	
Taxable estate	$2,500,000	Pre-gift estate	$2,500,000
Federal estate tax	823,750	Taxable gift	$1,000,000
Net estate to heirs	$1,676,250	Gift tax paid	143,750
		Estate reduction	1,143,750
		Taxable estate	$1,356,250
		Federal estate tax	609,563
		Net estate to heirs	$ 746,687
		Plus: Gift	1,000,000
Total to heirs	$1,676,250	Total to heirs	$1,746,687

By making the gift and paying gift taxes, the gift tax of $143,750 was removed from Marti's estate. This resulted in $70,437 more of Marti's estate actually getting to Marti's children. And this result doesn't even take into account the benefit of keeping the post-gift appreciation and after-tax income on the $1 million out of Marti's taxable estate. One catch, however: *The gift must be made more than 3 years before death; otherwise, the gift taxes will be brought back into your estate.* In addition, this arrangement assumes that you're comfortable with the nontax consequences of making a large gift—a gift that will deplete your estate to some extent. Finally, there are two other offsetting factors to take into account: First, if the property you give away is highly appreciated, the recipient will ultimately pay capital gains tax when he or she sells the property. This compares to an heir of an estate who gets the property with a cost basis that is equal to the property's value at the time of the decedent's death. Second, when you pay gift tax, you lose the time value of money on the tax paid. Overall, however, saving estate tax at rates up to 55% beats paying capital gains tax at a 20% federal rate. ■

Gifts to Minors

As noted earlier, only gifts of present interests qualify for the $10,000 gift tax exclusion. This generally means that the gifted property must be subject to the beneficiary's immediate enjoyment.

In the case of a parent's gift to a minor child, some legal and practical problems arise: The child typically can't manage his or her own affairs. Moreover, parents usually don't want to give their young children unfettered control over property. In fact, state laws frequently discourage outright gifts to minors. Such laws commonly prohibit or discourage the registration of securities in the name of a minor, for instance, and impose supervisory restrictions upon the sale of a minor's property. Gifts to minors can take different forms and affect the $10,000 annual gift tax exclusion differently.

Here are some ways in which gifts are typically made to minors:

- Outright gifts
- Guardianship
- Custodial arrangements
- Present interest trust
- Crummey trust
- Totten trust

Outright Gifts

Outright gifts to minors are treated as completed gifts. The $10,000 annual gift tax exclusion is available unless the donated property is itself a future interest. Income from the property is taxed to the minor, and the property can be included in the minor's estate. Because of the kiddie tax, however, your child—if under age 14—would generally be taxed at your rates on income over $1,400 from the property.

10 Big Mistakes in Estate Planning — #7
Saving the unified credit to shelter estate assets at your death

Keep in mind that the estate tax exclusion also applies to gifts you make during your lifetime, and can thereby be used to remove post-gift appreciation from your estate.

Guardianship

Property held in a guardianship arrangement is under the guardian's legal control subject to formal (and possibly burdensome) accounting to a court. The gift, income, and estate tax consequences are the same as for outright gifts. Thus, such gifts qualify for the $10,000 gift tax exclusion.

Custodial Arrangements

To overcome the legal disability minors have in owning property outright, all 50 states, the District of Columbia, and the Virgin Islands have adopted the Uniform Gifts (or Transfers) to Minors Act. Under this act, a custodian may hold both cash and securities for the minor until he or she reaches adulthood. Securities may be registered in the name of any bank, trust company, or adult as custodian for the minor. Custodial gifts to minors are completed gifts for gift tax purposes, and the annual gift tax exclusion is available. The income from the gift property during the custodial period is taxable to the minor (subject to kiddie tax provisions). However, income used for your minor child's maintenance and support is taxable to you as the person legally obligated to support the minor *whether or not you are the donor or custodian.*

In general, you should not act as custodian of your own gift to your minor child. The reason: If you die before your child becomes an adult, the current value of your gift will be included in your estate. Instead, your spouse may be the custodian. If you and your spouse are taking advantage of gift-splitting, consider making a third party the custodian.

 Q: Can I designate one person to provide my child's day-to-day care, and another person to look after her financial well-being?

 A: Definitely. The first person is the *guardian*; the second is the *trustee*. The determining factor should be who will best represent your child's interests. Obviously, a good working relationship between the two would be an advantage as well.

Present Interest Trust

Congress has enacted special rules to provide a well-defined method of making gifts to minors that qualify for the annual exclusion. The Internal Revenue Code provides that a gift to a qualifying trust established for an individual under the age of 21 will be considered a gift of a present interest and thus qualify for the $10,000 annual gift tax exclusion. The trust instrument must provide that the gift property and its income:

- May be expended for the benefit of the beneficiary before reaching age 21, and
- To the extent that it's not expended, will pass to the beneficiary upon becoming age 21.

The child must have the right to receive the assets of the trust at age 21. However, the trust assets don't have to be paid automatically to the child upon reaching age 21. It's acceptable if the child is given the *power* to withdraw everything for a period of 30 or 60 days, and is notified of the power. After the withdrawal period expires, the property stays in the trust and is administered according to the terms of the original trust. If the child dies before reaching age 21, the funds must be payable to the child's estate or as the child may appoint under a general power of appointment.

(*Note:* This Internal Revenue Code provision applies to trusts for children under the age of 21 even if a state law has reduced the age of majority to age 19 or 18.)

A present interest trust is useful when accumulating income is desirable for nontax reasons. It may not be suitable for large gifts, however, because of the requirement that the trust funds be payable to (or at least withdrawable by) the minor upon reaching age 21. The child's access to the trust assets at age 21 is something you should carefully consider. Also, the trust income tax brackets will generally tax income retained in a trust more heavily than if it were distributed to a child. The top federal income tax bracket of 39.6% applies to trust income above only $8,350, while a single person can have income of $278,450 before reaching that rate.

Crummey Trust

A Crummey trust is a different type of trust, one to which you can transfer property and have the gift qualify for the annual gift tax exclusion. The distinguishing characteristic of a Crummey trust is that it gives the beneficiary the right to demand annual distributions from the trust equal to the lesser of either the amount of the contributions to the trust during the year or a specified amount (e.g., $5,000 or 5% of the trust's value). The beneficiary (or legal guardian) must be notified of the power to withdraw the trust corpus, although the power is permitted to lapse or terminate after a short period of time (such as 30 days). If, following notification that a contribution has been made, the beneficiary fails to make a demand during the window period, the right lapses for that year's contributions. To the extent that the beneficiary (or guardian) has the right to demand distribution of the year's contribution, that contribution is a present interest and therefore qualifies for the annual gift tax exclusion. In practice, the child beneficiary almost never exercises the power, not wishing to bite the hand that feeds him or her, and perhaps causing the gifts to stop. This unspoken threat is the reason that these types of trusts are sometimes called "broken-arm" trusts.

In all other respects, the Crummey trust is very flexible. Once the withdrawal power has lapsed, the trustee can be required to accumulate income until the child reaches a specified age. The trustee can be restricted to using trust assets and income for specific purposes (e.g., college expenses). The trust is also useful as a vehicle for permanently removing assets from the parents' gross estates.

Furthermore, for income tax purposes, the Crummey trust's income is taxed to the beneficiary (or beneficiaries) who allowed their withdrawal right to lapse. Therefore, once the beneficiaries are over 13 years old, the income will be taxed at their rates, which will avoid the punitive tax rates applied to trusts.

Totten Trust

An "in trust for" account or so-called "Totten trust" is created when a donor deposits his own money into a bank account for the benefit of a minor, then names himself as trustee. This is an informal and revocable arrangement under certain states' laws. Upon the donor-trustee's death, the funds avoid probate and pass directly to the minor. However, the trust isn't considered a separate entity for tax purposes because the donor retains complete control over any property in the trust. Accordingly, the donor will be taxed on the income as if the trust were not in existence. Also, assets in the trust account will be includible in the donor's estate.

GENERATION-SKIPPING TRANSFER TAX

An additional tax may apply to gifts or bequests that skip a generation. An example of a generation-skipping transfer is a gift of property directly from a grandparent to a grandchild (which effectively "skips" the intervening generation).

The *generation-skipping transfer tax* is designed to impose the equivalent of the gift or estate tax the intervening generation would have paid. On a direct gift from a grandparent to a grandchild, the generation-skipping tax generally represents the amount of tax that would have been owed if the property had first been transferred to the child, who then died, leaving the property to the grandchild.

However, while the estate tax has a progressive rate structure, the generation-skipping transfer tax is imposed at the maximum estate and gift tax rate of 55%. It's payable *in addition to* any estate or gift tax otherwise payable as a result of the transfer.

The generation-skipping transfer tax is a very significant, if not confiscatory, tax. Fortunately, most people will escape it. First, outright gifts to grandchildren that qualify for the $10,000 annual gift tax exclusion aren't subject to the generation-skipping transfer tax. Similarly, payments of tuition and medical expenses that avoid gift tax also avoid this tax. Second, and perhaps most important, each person is entitled to an aggregate $1 million exemption from the tax for lifetime transfers and transfers at death. Since a married couple can "gift-split," they can make up to $2 million in generation-skipping transfers without incurring the tax. And any subsequent appreciation on the transferred property will escape generation-skipping tax.

If you're wealthy, you can maximize your opportunity to avoid the imposition of this tax on transfers to grandchildren and later generations by allocating your available $1 million exemption to trust transfers made during your own lifetime. And if your living descendants are already well provided for, you may be interested in establishing a *dynasty trust*. As its name implies, the trust can provide a huge benefit for future descendants by sheltering assets from estate, gift, and generation-skipping taxes for several generations.

If your wills and revocable trusts were drafted before passage of the 1986 Tax Act, you should review them to determine if they need revision to minimize the impact of the generation-skipping transfer tax. A personal financial counselor can help with this review.

12

TRUSTS, LIFE INSURANCE, AND ESTATE "FREEZES"

Two other techniques that you should consider as part of your estate planning are:

- Trusts
- Estate "freezes"

Both of these techniques can provide flexibility for your estate and reduce the taxes that your family would have to pay following your death.

TRUSTS: THE MOST USEFUL PLANNING TOOL

Aside from a written plan itself, trusts are possibly the most useful personal financial planning tool. A trust is an arrangement under which one person or institution holds legal title to real or personal property for the benefit of another person or persons, usually under the terms of a written document setting forth all parties' rights and responsibilities. A trust can hold property set aside under the management of a competent trustee for the benefit of other persons, present and future, and often avoid some taxes that otherwise would have to be paid.

Our discussions of estate planning so far have already referred to various kinds of trusts. You can probably understand this subject best in terms of particular *kinds* of trusts designed to achieve certain limited goals. Two of the most basic types of trusts are *irrevocable trusts* and *revocable trusts*.

Irrevocable Trusts

As is evident in its name, an irrevocable trust may not be changed or revoked after you create it. This type of trust is usually created to remove property and its future income and appreciation from your estate. The present interest and Crummey trusts are irrevocable trusts. You might also use an irrevocable trust if you want to make a gift to someone but want to prevent that person from spending the assets too quickly. Another purpose for an irrevocable trust is to prevent a beneficiary's creditors—or even a child's spouse in a divorce action—from reaching the property.

Property placed in an irrevocable trust will not be removed from your estate if you retain certain interests or powers in the trust, such as a life income interest or the power to determine which beneficiaries will receive distributions. Furthermore, any transfer to an irrevocable trust will be subject to gift tax if you relinquish all control over the property. If someone else will receive the income from the trust currently, or if it's a present interest trust, the $10,000 annual gift tax exclusion can shield at least part of the transfer from gift tax.

Besides saving you estate tax, irrevocable trusts created for your children may provide a limited income tax benefit. The amount of this benefit depends on how much other income your children already receive and whether the kiddie tax applies to them. In addition, very strict rules minimize the type of control you or your spouse may keep over the trust without causing the income to be taxed to you. Finally, the income will be taxed to you if it's used to pay for an item that you're legally obligated to provide as support for the beneficiary.

Revocable Trusts

A revocable trust (also known as a *living trust*) is created during your lifetime, and you may amend or revoke it at any time. The trust instrument directs how the assets held by it are to be managed during your lifetime. It can also act very much like a will by instructing how its assets should be distributed after your death.

What distinguishes a revocable trust from other kinds of trust arrangements is that *you keep the power to reclaim the trust assets*. You can amend the terms of the trust or even terminate it altogether whenever you wish. This means that by setting up a revocable trust, you really haven't committed yourself to anything—at least until you die and the trust becomes irrevocable. For all practical purposes, you continue to own the trust property beneficially; the trust merely gets bare legal title.

Since you keep complete control over the trust and its assets, the property held in it will be included in your gross estate for estate tax purposes. Also, all income and deductions attributable to the property in the trust flow back to you. On the other hand, your retained control means that your contributing assets to the trust won't trigger gift tax. This is the case even though the trust names the beneficiaries who will take the property following your death. However, a gift *will* occur if you give up your power to revoke or amend the trust, or if income or principal is actually paid to someone else.

The Advantages of Revocable Trusts. There are essentially no tax advantages gained by establishing a revocable trust; however, there can be some real financial and administrative advantages, including:

- Avoiding probate
- Avoiding legal guardianship
- Relief from financial responsibility

Avoiding Probate

Revocable trust assets pass to the beneficiaries you name in the trust document and are not controlled by your will. This cuts out the costs and delays that arise in some states as part of the probate process. Unlike probate, the identity of beneficiaries and instructions for distributing estate property aren't part of the public record. This allows you to maintain your privacy.

For those owning real property located outside their state of domicile at the time of death, ancillary probate proceedings will generally be required by each state in which such realty is located. By placing this property into a revocable trust, your estate can escape these multiple probate proceedings.

Avoiding Legal Guardianship

If you become incapacitated, the assets kept in your living trust would be managed automatically by a trustee you named in the trust document. Otherwise, the determination of whether and to what extent you're disabled or incompetent and who is going to handle your affairs could be left to public and potentially costly guardianship proceedings. (Note: A durable power of attorney can also be an effective tool for prearranging the management of your affairs in the event you become incapacitated. See Chapter 13 in this regard.)

Relief from Financial Responsibility

If you desire, you can use an independent trustee immediately to relieve you of the details of managing your property and investments, recordkeeping chores, and preparation and filing of income tax returns. An *agency account* managed by a bank trust department can perform these functions, too, but it doesn't provide the other benefits of using a revocable trust.

The Disadvantages of Revocable Trusts. Predictably, revocable trusts have some drawbacks, too, and aren't suited to everyone. Among them are:

- Legal fees and expenses
- Uncertain savings
- Taxation of gifts made directly by a trustee
- Title issues

Legal Fees and Expenses

Expect to pay legal fees and other expenses, such as real estate recording fees, to set up the trust and transfer property to it. You will also owe recurring trustee and administrative charges if you use a corporate trustee in lieu of managing the trust yourself.

Uncertain Savings

Probate cost savings may not be dramatic when you use a revocable trust. Many states have adopted streamlined probate procedures; this means that probate for a variety of estates can be completed more easily and less expensively than in the past, often with minimal court supervision. Moreover, using a living trust won't necessarily save on other legal, accounting, and executor's fees paid to handle your estate. Whether your assets are held in a living trust or pass through probate, the same sort of work will generally be needed to value your assets, prepare federal and state tax returns, settle creditors' claims, and resolve disputes among beneficiaries.

Taxation of Gifts
Made Directly by a Trustee

When making $10,000 annual exclusion gifts from a revocable trust, it's a good idea to withdraw the money first and then make the gift in your own name. Due to a quirk in the law, the IRS has been able to include in the estate of a trust grantor gifts made directly by the trustee to a donee within 3 years preceeding the grantor's death. The same gift *outside* the trust is removed from the donor's estate as soon as the gift is completed.

10 Big Mistakes in Estate Planning—#8
Setting up a living trust instead of a will to reduce your estate tax bill

In fact, living trusts have no impact on your estate tax liability. Also, no one transfers *all* of their assets to a revocable trust. There will always be some assets held outside the
trust that will pass by state intestate laws without a will.

Title Issues

Finally, be sure that any property you want to have covered by the benefits of a revocable trust is legally titled
in the trustee's name. This is a straightforward point but
one that often ends up overlooked. It also means that after
you create the trust, you must remember to conduct
your personal business affairs through this vehicle. Doing so isn't difficult, but sometimes it becomes a burden.
Except for life insurance proceeds and property held
jointly with right of survivorship, which pass by operation
of law, property held outside the trust at your death will
still be subject to probate.

Life Insurance Trusts

Next to your home, life insurance policies may well be your most
valuable assets. You may not realize, however, that life insurance
proceeds payable to your estate will be included in your gross estate

for estate tax purposes. You may also not realize that merely retaining even one of the incidents of ownership (mentioned earlier) will cause the proceeds to be included in the estate—*regardless of who the policy's beneficiary may be.*

What's the solution to this problem? One possibility is that to minimize estate taxes, you shouldn't own any life insurance policies. This doesn't mean that you shouldn't *have* life insurance; rather, it means that by transferring the policy and all incidents of ownership to your children or to a trust for your family's benefit, you can reap significant tax advantages. However, to be effective in keeping the proceeds out of your estate, you must make the gift more than 3 years before you die. You can avoid the 3-year waiting period for a newly purchased policy if you take proper steps to have someone else (e.g., a trustee of an irrevocable trust) apply for the policy. An ideal way to structure these types of irrevocable life insurance trusts enables you to apply your annual gift tax exclusion to cover contributions of money you make each year to the trust for paying premiums. The trust can therefore be used as a powerful way to leverage the annual exclusion to get insurance proceeds to your heirs without income, gift, or estate tax.

How a Trust Can Save Taxes

Life insurance proceeds are free from *income* taxes when they're paid to your survivors. However, the death benefits on policies you own are included in your estate and can be taxed at a rate as high as 55% at the federal level. An irrevocable life insurance trust avoids estate taxes because it's a separate legal entity in which you retain no interest. Once you transfer assets to this type of trust, you forfeit all control and ownership rights and therefore relieve yourself of the resulting tax liabilities. The idea of the life insurance trust is therefore to remove the policy proceeds from your own and your spouse's taxable estates. Proper drafting can accomplish this goal while allowing your spouse to receive income for life and principal as needed. You can achieve similar estate tax benefits by assigning ownership of the policy to your children. However, this alternative obviously lacks the planning flexibility offered by a life insurance trust.

How They Work

A trustee manages the life insurance trust, maintaining the policy during your life by paying the premiums. At your death, the trustee receives the policy proceeds and acts in accordance with your instructions in the trust document. You could direct that the death benefits be distributed immediately to named beneficiaries. In addition to being free from estate taxes, the death benefits are paid to your survivors without the costs and delays of probate (i.e., estate settlement). Alternatively, you can have the trustee manage the life insurance proceeds after your death, disbursing the money to your survivors over a specified period of time.

10 Big Mistakes in Estate Planning — #9 Making no plans to shelter taxable life insurance proceeds

Since life insurance benefits may push your estate past the $625,000 mark (or push yours and your surviving spouse's combined estate past the $1.2 million mark), you should transfer ownership of the policy to your children or other heirs. Alternatively, you can fund a life insurance trust.

Transferring a Policy

You can create a life insurance trust by transferring an existing policy to an irrevocable trust. The transfer is considered a taxable gift, but the tax is calculated on the surrender value of the policy, which, for cash value-type policies, is most often substantially less than the death benefit. Term insurance policies can also be transferred with the gift amount being only the amount of the current year's premium paid in as of the transfer. The tax cost of transferring a policy during your lifetime could therefore be substantially less than the estate taxes due upon your death. (*Note:* If you die within 3 years of the transfer, the policy proceeds would be included in your taxable estate.)

Setting Up a Trust with a New Policy

You can also set up a trust and have the trustee apply for a new policy on your life. You can transfer cash to the trust each year to enable the trustee to make the premium payments. These cash transfers are taxable gifts unless beneficiaries are given withdrawal powers (i.e., Crummey powers) that annually total more than the premium payments. Because the trustee applied for a new policy in which you never had any ownership rights, the policy proceeds would not be included in your estate, even if you were to die within 3 years.

10 Big Mistakes in Estate Planning—#10

Not keeping your beneficiary designations up to date

You must name beneficiaries on many assets, including life insurance policies, retirement plans, and bank and brokerage accounts.

Once you create an irrevocable life insurance trust, it's carved in stone. You can't cancel or amend the trust or withdraw the assets. You also lose control over the life insurance policy, including the ability to borrow from or surrender the cash value or change the beneficiary. If you feel an irrevocable life insurance trust may serve your purposes, be sure to enlist the support of qualified professionals to draft and administer your trust. These arrangements require sophisticated tax and estate planning expertise. Ask about the costs to set up and administer the trust, but remember that these fees can be more than offset by the tax savings.

ESTATE FREEZE TECHNIQUES

Estate "freeze" techniques typically serve to fix the value of a business interest retained by a parent at its current value, while facilitating the transfer of the appreciating interest in the business at a low transfer tax cost. These techniques also serve to freeze the estate tax value of other assets expected to appreciate over time (e.g., real estate).

Recapitalizations have long been a favorite way to freeze a business's value, although they haven't been as advantageous since

Congress tightened the rules in 1990. Here's the scenario for a typical corporate recapitalization. First, the parent owning all of a company's stock exchanges his or her common stock for a combination of preferred and common stock. The parent then transfers the common stock to a younger generation while retaining the preferred shares. This enables the parent to retain control over the company and draw earnings out. Since common stock generally appreciates much more in value relative to preferred stock, the parent is able to fix the value of his or her interest in the business for estate tax purposes. Then, as the business grows in value, the common stock would appreciate in the child's hands—avoiding the estate tax that would have been paid on the appreciation in the parent's estate.

To prevent perceived abuses of this technique, Congress imposed strict gift tax valuation rules in the 1990 Tax Act. To minimize the gift tax incurred in transferring the common stock before 1990, the preferred stock that the parent retained was typically loaded up with liquidation, redemption, noncumulative dividend, and other rights. Adding such "bells and whistles" to the preferred stock would build up its value and correspondingly deflate the common stock's market value. With very little remaining value in the company to attach to the common stock, the common could be transferred to a child at a very low gift tax cost. Because these types of rights would rarely be exercised when common stock is held by family members, the tax law now treats them as worthless. The value of the common stock transferred—and the gift tax triggered—will consequently be significant unless more certain rights are attached to the preferred stock, such as a right of cumulative dividends. Nevertheless, you may still achieve significant benefits by removing any post-gift appreciation in excess of the yield on the preferred stock from the parent's estate.

Split-Interest Trust Transfers

Other useful estate freezing techniques involve *split-interest trust transfers*. These include the *Grantor Retained Annuity Trust* and the *Personal Residence Grantor Retained Interest Trust*.

Grantor Retained Annuity Trust (GRAT)

If you own an interest in a closely held business, or if you hold other assets expected to increase substantially in value—whether in corporate or partnership form—you may be able to save on gift and estate taxes by transferring all or part of your interest into a trust while retaining the right to a fixed annuity for a term of years. For example, you could transfer a $1,000,000 interest and keep the right to receive $100,000 (10%) a year for 10 years. When the term of the GRAT expires, ownership of the interest would pass to your children. Your gift is $1,000,000 less the present value of the 10-year annuity. You can reduce the taxable gift resulting from the trust transfer very close to zero by setting a high enough annuity payout rate in combination with an appropriate trust term.

The annual annuity is generally satisfied from cash generated by the property or the property itself. You realize transfer tax benefits from the GRAT if the assets transferred produce a total return in excess of the IRS-assumed rate of return used in valuing the annuity. Thus, when interest rates are low, or when the expected return on an asset is particularly high, the GRAT can be especially attractive because it provides a leveraged way to move a significant amount of the appreciation on business assets (or perhaps marketable securities) to your children at an insignificant gift tax cost.

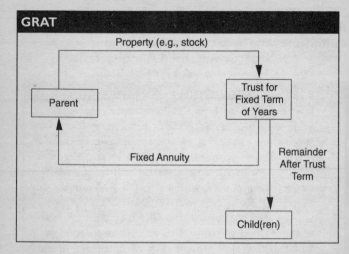

GRAT

Property (e.g., stock)

Parent

Trust for
Fixed Term
of Years

Fixed Annuity

Remainder
After Trust
Term

Child(ren)

Personal Residence Grantor Retained Interest Trust

The Personal Residence Grantor Retained Interest Trust (Residence GRIT) offers an opportunity to achieve significant gift and estate tax savings with virtually no risk. A Residence GRIT is an arrangement in which you transfer either a principal residence or vacation home to a trust, retaining (1) the right to income for a period of years (i.e., the right to live in the house during the trust term), and (2) the right to have the trust property returned to your estate if you die during the trust term. At the end of the trust term, the home goes to your children outright or remains in the trust for their benefit. The trust is irrevocable and the transfer is considered a gift of the present value of the property that will pass to your children in the future.

The GRIT offers transfer tax "leverage" because the amount of the gift for gift tax purposes will be considerably less than the current value of the home transferred to the trust.

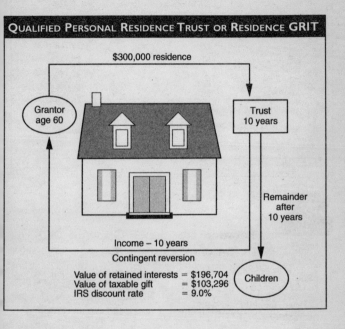

QUALIFIED PERSONAL RESIDENCE TRUST OR RESIDENCE GRIT

$300,000 residence

Grantor age 60

Trust 10 years

Remainder after 10 years

Income – 10 years

Contingent reversion

Value of retained interests = $196,704
Value of taxable gift   = $103,296
IRS discount rate   = 9.0%

Children

<table><tr><td>E
X
A
M
P
L
E</td><td>■ Let's say you're 60 years old. You transfer your home to a 10-year GRIT. The reportable gift is just over 34% of your home's value (assuming an IRS discount rate of 9.0%), as shown in the illustration below. For a $300,000 home, the gift would be $103,296—only a fraction of the $600,000 unified credit equivalent. If your home appreciates 3% per year during the 10-year trust term, there will be $403,175 of value passing to your children at the end of the 10 years—close to four times the amount of the taxable gift. ■</td></tr></table>

RESIDENCE GRITs— TAXABLE GIFT PER $100,000 OF VALUE OF HOUSE*

Age	Trust Term	Value of Taxable Gift
40	25	$ 9,420
45	20	13,305
50	15	23,129
55	12	29,718
60	10	34,432
65	8	40,141
70	5	54,090
75	5	49,409
80	3	60,972
83	3	56,532

*Assume IRS discount rate of 9.0%.

PLANNER In the case of both the GRAT and the GRIT, it's important to select a trust term that you expect to survive. That's because the property will be included in your estate at its date-of-death value if you die during the trust term. Nevertheless, there's really no downside tax risk to the GRAT or GRIT, since if death *did* occur during the term, you'd merely end up where you would have been had the GRAT or GRIT never been done. If you've already used up your unified credit and owe gift tax when you create the trust, death during the trust term would cause you to lose the time value of money on the gift tax paid. By surviving at least three years, this would be more than offset by your savings resulting from removing the gift tax from your taxable estate. (See pages 248–249.) Your financial advisor can provide more information on reducing transfer taxes with GRITs and GRATs.

Buy–Sell Agreements

Another way of attempting to fix the estate tax value of a business interest is to use a buy–sell agreement. Buy–sell agreements can actually fulfill three objectives:

First, the *buy–sell agreement can ensure that inside parties will retain control of a closely held business.* For example, a buy–sell agreement may prohibit the acquisition of closely held business stock by relatives, employees, or outsiders who are inactive or incapable of running the business. Thus management control can be retained by those most capable of managing the business.

Second, *a buy–sell agreement can ensure that your heirs can dispose of your interest in a closely held business at a fair price when you die.* In this way, the agreement provides a source of liquidity for the shareholders' estate.

Third, *a valid and binding buy–sell agreement can be used to try to fix the estate tax value of stock in a closely held business.* This used to be accomplished by fixing the future price of the stock at a reasonable fixed amount or by basing the sales price on a formula. However, buy–sell agreements among family members that are entered into after October 8, 1990, will not control the estate tax valuation of a business interest unless evidence (such as actual agreements in other businesses) can be produced that unrelated parties would enter into a similar agreement.

Note: A critical element of a successful valuation freeze involves obtaining an expert appraisal of the property that takes advantage of all available discounts and yet will be likely to withstand an IRS challenge. A valuation professional can perform valuations of businesses, real estate, or other assets for transfer tax or other purposes.

13

ESTATE LIQUIDITY, POWERS OF ATTORNEY, AND LIVING WILLS

Now for some Last Things—in this case, three topics to conclude our discussion of estate planning, plus a reminder.

- Estate liquidity
- Durable powers of attorney
- Living wills and health care powers of attorney
- The importance of periodic review

ESTATE LIQUIDITY: RAISING CASH TO PAY DEATH TAXES

If you own a closely held business, your estate may not have sufficient cash to pay all the estate's obligations, including estate taxes, following your death. Indeed, the principal estate asset may be the business itself. Without sufficient liquidity, the estate may be forced to sell a portion of the business to raise enough cash to satisfy these obligations. The techniques described below can help alleviate liquidity problems. These techniques are *stock redemptions to pay death taxes and installment payment of estate tax.*

Stock Redemptions to Pay Death Taxes

A special tax law provision—Section 303 of the Internal Revenue Code—allows a tax-favored redemption of stock where the decedent owned a substantial interest in a closely held business. Absent the special rule, the redemption might be treated as a dividend, meaning that the entire payment for the stock would be income to the estate. Assuming that the technical requirements of this provision are met, the redemption will be given capital gain treatment. This is a real benefit in this situation because the estate will have a new basis in the decedent's stock equal to its fair market value at the date of the death. The result is that only post-death appreciation will be taxed upon the redemption, and only up to the maximum capital gains tax rate of 28%.

To qualify for a Section 303 redemption, the value of all the corporation's stock included in the decedent's gross estate must exceed 35% of the decedent's adjusted gross estate. The adjusted gross estate is the gross estate less the allowable deductions for funeral and administration expenses, debts, and certain losses (but before any charitable deduction or marital deduction).

A qualifying redemption under Section 303 is limited in amount to the sum of the following items:

- Federal and state death taxes
- Funeral expenses
- Estate administration expenses

An estate doesn't actually have to be illiquid for Section 303 to apply. In other words, an estate may take advantage of the provisions of Section 303 and redeem stock up to the maximum amount referred to above, even if the estate otherwise has sufficient liquid assets to take care of its expenses and taxes. It's often desirable to redeem stock under Section 303 because it may be difficult for your heirs to withdraw funds from the corporation without paying tax at ordinary income rates.

PLANNER Installment Payment of Estate Tax

To further relieve the tax burden on an estate holding a closely held business, your heirs can pay estate taxes attributable to your interest in such a business over a 14-year period if certain conditions are met. This 14-year pay-out offers a favorable interest rate plus a 5-year deferral of the first installment of estate taxes. The tax is then paid in 10 installments. This deferral provision only applies to an "interest in a closely held business." To qualify for the 14-year payout, the value of the closely held business must exceed 35% of the adjusted gross estate.

The amount of estate tax that qualifies for a deferred payout is limited to the portion of the total tax that is attributable to the business interest. For example, if the decedent's qualifying stock constitutes 62% of the adjusted gross estate, 62% of the total estate tax liability may be deferred.

The executor of an estate owning a qualified business interest who makes the election to defer payment will pay none of the tax attributable to the business interest for 5 years. However, interest on the tax for the first 4 years must be paid annually. After the fifth year of deferral, the estate tax liability must begin to be paid with interest in up to 10 yearly installments.

A favorable rate of 4% is charged on the deferred estate tax attributable to the first $1 million in value of the closely held business interest. The regular federal interest rate applies to the deferred estate tax in excess of that amount.

Durable Powers of Attorney

Suppose that you've prepared a valid will to provide for the proper management and disposition of your estate after you die. It's safely tucked away. Now you can relax, right? Maybe so. If you were to suffer an illness or injury, however, you might end up incapable of managing your financial affairs. Under such circumstances, the will you've so thoughtfully prepared won't help a bit.

Confronting your disability, your family might have to have a court appoint a guardian or conservator for you so that your finances continue to be properly managed. That could mean delays, legal expenses, and perhaps public disclosure of your infirmity. Meanwhile, your bills and taxes might remain unpaid. Couldn't your spouse just step in and take over for you? Often, that's not possible. He or she wouldn't have the legal authority to perform certain acts on your behalf. As a result, your family might end up in a state of financial limbo until the courts granted a guardianship or conservatorship.

The Simple Alternative

■ **TIP:** The good news is that there's a simple alternative to guardianship. A *durable power of attorney* is one of the safest, simplest, and cheapest ways of continuing the management of your affairs in the event of your incapacity. It's a short legal document that your lawyer prepares, stating simply that you (the *principal*) grant authority to one or more individuals [*your attorney(s)-in-fact*] to manage your financial affairs (and personal affairs such as health care, if you wish) on your behalf.

You retain the right to modify or revoke the power at any time. The document terminates automatically on your death. One caveat: If you do revoke the power without informing third parties (e.g., a bank), they can continue to rely on the directions of your attorney-in-fact without penalty. Also, if a guardian is appointed for you, that guardian can revoke the power just as you yourself could have.

The power is *durable* because the underlying document creating it specifically states that it remains in force even if you become disabled or incapacitated. This feature is what gives the power its value in ensuring continuity of your financial management. ■

General and Special Powers

Your durable power of attorney can be as broad or as narrow as you wish. A *general durable power* grants your attorney-in-fact the authority to handle virtually all financial matters that you would ordinarily manage yourself. If you prefer, you can grant a *special durable power*, under which the attorney-in-fact's authority is restricted to one or more specific functions designated by you. The general power is better designed to avoid the problem of guardianship.

If you own a business, you might execute two durable powers with separate attorneys-in-fact: a spouse or other close relative to handle your personal affairs, and a business associate or trusted advisor to handle your business. The underlying document could provide that the latter receives a fee for services.

Springing Powers

Typically, a durable power takes effect when it is created, so that the designated attorney-in-fact can assume responsibility as soon as it becomes necessary. To be sure that control is not assumed prematurely, you may want to give the underlying document to your lawyer or accountant for safekeeping, since your attorney-in-fact cannot legally act for you without possession of the document.

Another way you might deal with the problem of premature exercise is through a *springing durable power*, which is worded so that it becomes effective only in the event of your disability. One drawback to the springing power, however, is this: While all 50 states and the District of Columbia recognize durable powers, the validity of a springing power is unclear in some states and specifically denied in a few others.

Another problem is that since its operation is triggered (or sprung) by disability, it could be difficult in some cases to convince the attorney-in-fact that disability has actually occurred and that it's safe to begin acting for the principal. Thus the document must contain a clear definition of disability: for example, certification by two designated physicians.

Combining Durable Powers and Revocable Trusts

As we discussed in Chapter 12, revocable trusts can provide for the management of your assets during life and after death. Revocable trusts can also provide the same benefit in the event of disability.

PLANNER Under these circumstances, you don't even have to fund the trust fully. You can create it with a nominal amount (say, $10) and make it available as a *standby trust*. The durable power of attorney can be drafted to direct the powerholder to fund the trust with selected assets, or with your entire estate, if you become incapacitated.

Options

As principal, you can authorize your attorney-in-fact to do any number of things in your stead, limited only by the laws of your state. For example, you can give your attorney-in-fact the power to continue implementing your plan to reduce the size of your estate with annual tax-free gifts to your heirs (see Chapter 10 regarding gift tax). You can also provide for charitable donations, payment of medical bills, and tuition disbursements. Note that absent *explicit* authorization in the document, the powerholder will not have the legal authority to make gifts on your behalf under most state laws.

Here are other tasks your attorney-in-fact can perform for you:

- Manage your investment portfolio
- Forgive or collect debts owed to you
- File tax returns and pay taxes
- Represent you in legal matters
- Manage your business
- Provide for your medical care

Two Caveats. Some financial institutions (e.g., banks and brokerage houses) will honor *only* powers executed on forms that their own staffs have prepared; you may need to create more than one document to cover all needs. Also, one thing your attorney-in-fact cannot do is change your will.

Choosing Your Attorney-in-Fact

It goes without saying that the person you choose as your attorney-in-fact must be someone you trust completely. This person should also have some knowledge of financial matters—especially if you contemplate a general power. Ideally, your attorney-in-fact should also have some understanding of your financial objectives so as to be better equipped to carry out your plans. Accordingly, spouses often name each other as their attorneys. Whomever you pick for this important task, you should designate an alternate as well, since your first choice may be unavailable when the time comes. Finally, your attorney-in-fact must be of legal age when the power is exercised.

Can one of my relatives challenge the legality of my appointing another relative to be my attorney-in-fact?

 Someone can certainly *challenge* the legality of the appointment, but doing so successfully is another matter. Provided that your durable power of attorney is properly written and executed, your wishes would stand up in court

Spread the Word

A durable power of attorney is especially important for aged parents and older close relatives. You should encourage these relatives to consider a durable power in your favor to relieve you of a significant burden if and when they are unable to shoulder their own responsibilities. Here's an example: Your widowed parent suddenly becomes incapacitated and is unable to write checks. Without a durable power in place, you might have to pay the bills out of your own pocket, at least temporarily, and you would be powerless to make other important decisions on your parent's behalf.

A durable power of attorney won't solve all your financial management problems, but it can certainly reduce the physical, psychological, and financial burdens that will fall on your family if you became disabled. And the durable powers for which you are attorney-in-fact will do the same for older members of your family. *Note:* Although some form of this financial planning tool exists throughout the United States, the state laws aren't identical. Consult your legal advisor before proceeding.

LIVING WILLS AND HEALTH CARE POWERS OF ATTORNEY

You may recall that during the final weeks of his life, former President Richard Nixon refused "heroic measures" and received only palliative (discomfort-easing) care at his home in New Jersey.

Similarly, former First Lady Jacqueline Kennedy Onassis refused life-prolonging medical intervention before her death from non-Hodgkins lymphoma. Former President Nixon and Mrs. Onassis both retained control over their final medical care through use of a *living will* and a *health care power of attorney*.

Perhaps you've reflected on your own wishes if you were to face a similar situation. Although no one likes to imagine the possibility of being in such a helpless state, the statistical possibility of such an event remains fairly high. This is why it's wise to ensure that your wishes will be respected if you become incapacitated.

Documents That Declare Your Wishes

Living wills and durable health care powers of attorney (some-times called *health care proxies* or *medical powers of attorney*) are legal instruments similar to durable powers of attorney. Their pur-pose is to make sure that your wishes regarding health care issues will be carried out.

A *living will* is a statement that allows you to specify clearly your wishes concerning life-sustaining medical treatment. In this way, a court has evidence of your wishes regarding the refusal of medical treatment. The living will describes what sort of physical condition you wish to trigger the document's provisions, and it lists the types of treatments you wish to avoid.

A *durable health care power of attorney* picks up where the living will leaves off. It's an instrument through which you can appoint a person to make medical and health care decisions on your behalf in the event of your temporary or permanent in-capacity. It's called a *durable* power because it remains valid and operative despite any subsequent incapacity you may suffer. You direct the designated powerholder to make decisions based on your previously expressed wishes—or, in the absence of a clear expression, to act in your best interests based on what this person knows about you.

Most states have enacted legislation recognizing both living wills and some form of durable health care powers of attorney.

Because each state's legal requirements may differ for proper execution of these documents, you should consult a lawyer familiar with the rules in your state. If you live in a state that lacks legislation on these instruments, it's still crucial for you to state your wishes in writing as completely and explicitly as possible. Explicitness may also be necessary if you later take up residence in a state other than the one in which you drafted the document. If you split your time between two states during the year, you may need to draft *two* living wills and durable health care powers of attorney; this will provide documents that comply with each state's requirements.

Q: Do medical personnel really follow the wishes you state in health care powers-of-attorney and living wills? Aren't they too scared of lawsuits to comply?

A: Many states now regard a living will as a legal document. Medical practitioners are more likely than before to follow your wishes as stated in your living will. However, not all physicians or institutions are equally responsive either to the general concept of the living will or to specific provisions. You should discuss in detail all your views on the situation with your attorney and with your doctor.

Why You Should Have Both

Because a living will can't cover every circumstance, the extra step of executing a durable health care power of attorney will help assure that the powerholder will carry out your intentions to the extent that the living will doesn't specifically define them. The powerholder you select should be someone you have complete confidence in, of course, since this person will have broad powers to deal with unanticipated circumstances. The ideal person is someone who knows you well enough to have a clear idea of your preferences in such a situation.

You should update your living will and durable health care power of attorney periodically to reflect any change in your intentions. Updating is also generally advisable every couple of years so that a judge or a hospital will regard them as accurately expressing your current thinking. You reduce the threat of someone challenging the validity of a living will or durable health care power of attorney when you keep the document current.

Implementation

Here are some steps to follow if you're concerned enough to take action:

Step 1. Reflect on your wishes regarding medical treatment and discuss them with your doctor and family.

Step 2. Properly execute a living will. With your attorney's help, be as clear as possible about your intentions in a variety of circumstances.

Step 3. Execute *two* originals of a durable power of attorney authorizing someone to make medical decisions for you in the event of your incapacity. Give one of the originals to the appointee.

Step 4. Give appropriate doctors a copy of each document and emphasize your specific wishes to them.

Step 5. Inform your family members of these documents, tell them the contents, and make sure the documents are accessible to them in a time of urgent need. In other words, don't keep your documents locked away.

Step 6. From time to time, you should update your living will and durable power of attorney.

> Besides providing you with the ability to control more aspects of your medical care (not to mention the possibility of sparing your family the pain of a prolonged ordeal) these documents can indirectly help to preserve your estate for your heirs. If you have clarified that you don't want artificial support systems to prolong your life, there's less danger that escalating medical care expenses will drain your estate.

■ **TIP:** For more information about living wills, contact the National Council for the Right to Die, 200 Varick Street, 10th floor, New York, NY 10014. Phone: (212) 366-5540. ■

PERIODIC REVIEW AND FOLLOW-UP

In light of the frequent changes in all phases of taxation in recent years, a periodic review of your personal financial plan makes common sense. Filing an annual income tax return forces most taxpayers to look over their situations at least once a year; however, many people—perhaps most—allow years to go by without adequately considering possible changes in property holdings or key provisions in wills and trust instruments. Inflation and increased life insurance coverage push a large number of unaware families into high estate tax brackets.

The Six Basic Considerations

To be safe, you should reappraise the following six basic tax and financial considerations from time to time.

One: Tax Laws and Rulings. Have there been any changes in the tax laws or rulings that might affect your present estate plan adversely?

Two: Liquidity. Does your estate have sufficient liquidity to take care of debts, taxes, funeral expenses, and estate administration expenses?

Three: Family Circumstances. Have there been any changes in your family's circumstances (such as births, adoptions, deaths, marriages, illness or disability, special schooling needs, etc.) that might call for revisions in the estate plan?

Four: Gifts. Should a gift program be initiated or continued? Which assets are most appropriate for such a gift program?

Five: Ownership of Family Property. Is the present form of ownership of family property suitable for flexibility and savings in taxes and expenses?

Six: Forms of Payment and Designation. Has the proper form of payment and beneficiary designation been selected for distributions from qualified employee benefit plans?

What many people overlook in their personal financial planning is the opportunity to make lifetime gifts that take advantage of available exclusions. Too often, people also ignore the desirability of separating most jointly owned property because of tax and administrative considerations. The result of inaction is often one of paying taxes that could have been minimized.

Checklist for a Follow-Up

To jog your thinking, take a look at the following checklist for follow-up.

CHECKLIST FOR FOLLOW-UP

☐ If any adult member of your family doesn't have a will, or if any wills haven't been reviewed within the last 3 years, contact your CPA or your attorney. This is especially important in light of the frequency of tax legislation.

☐
☐ Compile a record location schedule of all important financial and legal papers and inform all appropriate persons of its location.

☐ Compile information on the cost and approximate purchase date of all your assets, including your residence.

☐ If you haven't already done so, be sure that your spouse or whomever you designate as your personal representative knows your attorney, CPA, trust officer, broker, insurance advisor, and other appropriate persons.

☐ To reduce federal estate taxes, consider assigning ownership rights of your group-term life insurance to your spouse, a trust, or other appropriate recipient.

☐ Review the beneficiary designations for your employee retirement or Keogh plan and other employee benefits.

☐ Review the disposition of your property not subject to probate (jointly owned property, life insurance) to determine if you have overfunded the marital deduction.

☐
☐ Make sure that you've provided for the legal guardianship and personal custody of your minor children.

☐ Review your wills or trust instruments with your attorney to ascertain whether the provisions, if any, concerning simultaneous death produce the desired marital deduction result.

☐
☐ If you and your spouse don't have durable powers of attorney, consider having them drawn up soon.

CHECKLIST FOR FOLLOW-UP (continued)

Special Problems Alert

If your answer to any of the following questions is yes, you may need assistance to determine whether there are tax problems on the horizon. Remember: *A yes is a warning flag but not necessarily a signal that there is a problem.*

Are you:

Making significant cash gifts to members of your family that are likely to continue indefinitely?

Planning to make gifts to grandchildren within the next few years? In your will?

Anticipating a significant inheritance? Is your spouse?

Do you:

Hold assets jointly with your spouse, other than your residence and a working banking account?

Have a simple will that leaves all property you own at the date of your death outright to your spouse?

Own any real property in a state other than the state of your residence?

Have a child or other relative with a serious medical problem that may require special consideration in your will or trust instrument?

Need relief from the management of your investments?

Have substantially more or less property than your spouse?

Have you:

Moved your residence to a different state since you last executed your will?

Named your estate as the beneficiary of your life insurance or your retirement plan benefits?

Lived a part of your married life in a community property state?

291

INDEX

MONEYOPOLIS ℠

A Public Service of Ernst & Young's
Financial Education Program

w w w . m o n e y o p o l i s . o r g

Ξ ERNST & YOUNG LLP